THE CRAFT OF
painting on
GLASS

THE CRAFT OF
painting on
GLASS

MATERIALS, TECHNIQUES AND IDEAS
by Delian Fry

Photography by Amanda Heywood

Little, Brown and Company
Boston New York Toronto London

A Little, Brown Book

First published in Great Britain in 1996
by Little, Brown and Company

Copyright © Delian Fry

A CIP catalogue record for this book is available
from the British Library

ISBN 0-316-87565-1

Design by Janet James
Technical Editor: Judith Casey

10 9 8 7 6 5 4 3 2 1

Typeset by Peter Coombs
Printed and bound in Italy by Graphicom

Little, Brown and Company (UK)
Brettenham House
Lancaster Place
London WC2E 7EN

THE CRAFT OF painting on GLASS

contents

introduction

COLOUR, light and design are the essential ingredients of painting on glass. The effect of sunshine, streaming through a dazzling bouquet of summer poppies, or a twinkling array of painted glass angels on the Christmas tree, entrance and delight the eye. We have all seen stained-glass panels in churches, public buildings, front doors and windows and thought how wonderful they were, but not exactly within our capabilities to construct. Nowadays, with the development of non-firing glass paint, especially made for painting on glass, everyone can design and create stained-glass projects. These can range from small sun catchers, painted roundels, exotic recycled glass jars and vases to Tiffany-style lampshades and window panels with top leading.

Ten years ago, when I started **GETTING STARTED** painting on glass as a development of my stained-glass window making, I was looking for something different, a medium in which I could express my interest in line and colour and light. The freedom of getting away from the leaded line and the constrictions of size, combined with the arrival of non-firing paints, directed me towards painting on glass instead.

At first it was difficult getting hold of glass paints, but now, this craft can be enjoyed practically anywhere, for only a modest outlay, with highly satisfying results. Many of my students have gone on to produce and sell original works.

At first, I experimented on all sorts of glass objects and devised lots of interesting treatments for many everyday items, such as vases, plates, dishes, wine glasses, glass lamp shades and old mirrors. Most satisfying was the idea of rescuing discarded glass and turning it into fantastical treasures and useful artifacts. I found that the colours of glass paints could be deep and jewel-like or as light as a fairy's wing, depending on the medium. The sheer versatility of glass paints gave me enormous satisfaction as an artist and I found I could create a wide range of ingenious and exciting glass art projects.

Although work can be produced that looks remarkably like traditional stained-glass windows, it is much more fun to develop an entirely new way of using colour on glass. The really interesting aspect of glass painting is that anyone, young or old, skilled or unskilled can produce something good to look at. This goes for five-year-olds painting on jam jars to adults letting loose on their stored up glass vases!

The basic materials for this craft are **THE BASICS** simply cut the acrylic into shape with a glass and paint. A visit to your local glass merchant should meet your needs. They often have machines that can cut circles, squares or oval blanks.

Good places to look for glass-ware are, of course, car-boot sales, yard sales and jumble sales, and high-street stores often have plain glass jars and containers in their kitchenware department. It's worth asking older friends and relatives to look in cupboards for long-forgotten glass dishes, vases, jugs and lamps. Some of the pressed glass bowls, jugs and dessert dishes made in the thirties and forties are great subjects to paint and decorate and may even have embossed designs already 'built in'. Bottles and jars are excellent subjects for conversion projects. Old mayonnaise jars and pickle jars are good for painting and top-leading and, if you know a pub or bar owner, he or she may have a wide collection of interesting bottles. Look for liqueur bottles that have impressed designs. In fact anything made from glass which looks fun to paint.

Another good source of glass for recycling is replacement window companies as they quite often take out whole windows and throw them away. The old windows make wonderful ready-made hanging glass window panels, already framed. Just screw in some eye hooks and hang them. If you do not wish to use glass but would like to make your own roundels, you can use sheet acrylic, available from DIY stores. You Stanley knife. Several mail-order craft companies have a range of ready-cut acrylic and glass blanks, in circles and ovals.

For glass painting you don't need lots of expensive equipment. For those who can draw and design it is fun to create new ideas. The less gifted should use the pattern library in this book or keep a design-idea folder and collect cards, gardening books and colouring books or even wrapping paper. Children's colouring books are ideal as they have strong but simple design lines. The intrinsic design of many glass items often acts as inspiration, especially among the junior artists. A curved vinegar bottle, washed and stripped of its label, becomes a dolphin or sinuous salmon. Or a chunky honey jar, painted in rainbow stripes, converts into a magical nightlight.

You will need glass paints, which are available from many good art and craft stores and also by mail order (See Suppliers and Stockists). There are several manufacturers who produce a wide range of colours and mediums. For drawing the design onto glass you will also need a special outliner. The intention is to simulate a leaded glass outline such as you would get using a traditional lead came. It is important that the outliner dries thoroughly before attempting to paint the glass. Imagine that you are colouring the layers of a trifle! To get the best result wait for the layers to dry before moving on to the next one.

You will need a flat surface to work on, and a light and airy room if possible. The spirit- and acetate-based glass paints especially need good ventilation. You will also need plain newsprint, white paper, and lots of rags and kitchen roll, as well as drawing paper, felt-tip pens and pencils for your designs. Later on you will need to acquire stick-on lead, glass glue, copper foil, solder, flux and a stained-glass, hobby soldering iron. Most of these items can be found at a stained-glass suppliers, or local hardware and DIY stores.

CREATING YOUR DESIGN

When it comes to design do not feel that it is beyond your talents. With the use of copying machines and a good supply of colouring books, plus a little imagination, you will be able to create a really striking piece of glass. The ideal design to look for is quite simple, with an outline in black, and there are many themes to choose from. Sometimes museums have colouring books of wild flowers and specific subjects, such as pub signs or advertising logos. I have two excellent colouring books of old Celtic and medieval manuscripts with intricate black-and-white line drawings of angels and exotic beasts. These would look wonderful as painted panels or used on small roundels for Christmas. Greetings cards have all sorts of useful subjects: animals, flowers and even the script can be saved for future use on birthday or christening roundels. Wrapping papers have some good designs and wallpaper books have a useful selection of flowers and borders. I keep a huge collection of magazines, wallpaper, cards, gardening catalogues, even bits of curtain material, to provide me with a library of design ideas and references. I was once asked to do a front door featuring the leaves and flowers of the Chinese Strawberry tree. I was able to do this by finding it in a gardening catalogue and blowing it up in size so that I could see the shape of the leaves and flowers and the catalogue also gave me an accurate reference for the colour.

For the past five years I have been giving classes in glass painting to all sorts of interested students. In schools I have worked with quite young children between the ages of 6 and 13, and they have all enjoyed themselves hugely. The water-based glass paints are usually best for this age group, and they have great fun painting jars and bottles as well as making roundels and trying some stencil glass painting. Older students can easily manage larger projects such as door and window panels. I have also explored glass painting with an arts-therapy organisation, teaching and helping people who wish to learn a new craft.

The Isle of Wight, where I live, is positively twinkling with roundels and painted glass *objets d'art* and the sales of glass paint have quadrupled. The only glass items not to paint on please, are the glass milk bottles from the dairy as these should be returned for re-use.

So, remember that there are at least ten windows in your home, not to mention empty jars, mirrors, bottles, vases… all made of glass!

m a t e r i a l s

Most glass merchants are extremely **GLASS**
obliging and informative when it comes to
supplying glass for painting. Many have off-cut
bins with free, or very cheap, glass for those
who can cut their own blanks. However, there
are machines for cutting and grinding glass
circles (roundels), squares and ovals, and it is
easy to get your roundels and panels cut exactly
to size. It is a good idea to ask for the edges to
be ground, to save cutting your fingers. As oil is
used to cut glass, remember to clean the glass
well before attempting to paint on it.

Flat glass usually comes in 2mm, 4mm or
6mm (⅛, ¼ or ⅜ in) plate thickness. It is called
'Float' glass. 2mm or 4mm is quite satisfactory
for painting. But for doors you must use 6mm
laminated glass or toughened (reinforced) glass.
This is a legal requirement for glass doors, for
safety reasons. If in doubt, ask a glazier who is a
member of the Glass and Glazing Federation.
They should have the latest regulations at hand
and can tell you the correct glass to use for
particular windows and doors and even roofs. If
you are transporting the glass home in your car,
wrap it up well and put it in the boot of the
car. If that is not possible then place it on the
floor of the car, again well wrapped. If the car
has to stop suddenly you don't want glass loose
inside the car.

You can create terrific refractive effects by
painting on 'bumpy' glass, commonly used
to obscure bathroom windows. This is called
'Flemish' glass and has both large and small
bumps, rather like irregular waves. Pilkingtons
have a range of decorative and embossed glass
that can be incorporated into designs, among
these are sailing boats, wavy lines and assorted
granular effects that can look quite spectacular
when painted with a 'Monet' paint effect (see
the Monet's Waterlilies panel).

Ready-made glass items for painting fall into
two categories: new and recycled glass. New
glass includes cheap wine glasses and decanters
found at any home store, glass plates, or
embossed glass plates with fish or similar
patterns embossed on the glass. A very effective
window hanging can be achieved by painting a
fish-embossed plate, gluing on a suitable glass
eye and attaching a hanging chain using the
copper-foil border method, described in the
practical workshop section of this book.
Recycled glass can be found in cupboards, junk
shops, car-boot sales, yard sales and charity shops:
look for old glasses, jars and bottles, embossed
glass ice-cream dishes, old glass lampshades,
decrepit mirrors, and even glass condensers
from obsolete power lines. They look very dense
and solid and are usually ribbed in appearance.
But they make great terrariums, especially when
painted with jungle ferns and parrots.

There are three kinds of glass paints: **GLASS PAINTS** used in well-ventilated areas, and you water-based, spirit-based and acetate-based. can buy a special acetate cleaner in most hardware or DIY stores.

The water-based paints are ideal for the beginner and those who are not particularly well co-ordinated. They are also good for those who do not like to work with strong-smelling paints. They are usually cloudy when first applied, but dry to a clear finish.

Glass paints come in a good range of colours and, as long as you stick to the same medium, can be mixed and thinned as necessary.

The spirit-based paints should be used in a well-ventilated space and there should be plenty of rags and turps or white spirit to hand for cleaning up and spills.

It's a good idea to start off with a basic set of colours, red, yellow, blue, white and black, and learn to mix as many colours as you can. There are other secondary colours in most ranges, and a few rather unusual ones that are hard to mix. These are better kept for special projects if you are trying to keep the cost down.

The acetate-based paints should always be

These flat-based glass blobs are **GLASS JEWELS** a few jumble sales should produce available from home-decorating stores, in bags some suitable stones and beads for gluing onto or loose, and come in a myriad of colours. jars and bottles and lamps.

Otherwise mail order craft suppliers carry them and so do most stained-glass suppliers. Many glass blowers also make them for retail sale, otherwise a trawl through the junk jewellery at

If you use special glass glue which dries trans-parently, remember that it will not stick on glass paint, so leave unpainted the areas where jewels are to go.

This is for creating the bones of your **OUTLINER** effect. The gold and silver outliners are design. It comes in tubes and is made by the very good for adding decorative details, giving same companies that make the glass paint. It is definition to flower stamens and Christmas available in black, lead, silver and gold and items. They are particularly effective when sometimes in copper as well. You apply it decorating bottles, as they can be used for lots through the nozzle rather like toothpaste, so if of squiggles and dots and swirly features. you want a fine delicate outline, look for a fine Inscriptions and house names also look good in nozzle. There are some that are manufactured gold or silver, although it takes a bit of practice with thick nozzles to give a heavy leaded-light to control the flow of the outliner as you write.

This is used on painted panels, jars **STICK-ON LEAD** a special tool to press the lead tape and lamps to give the impression of a heavier leaded effect. It comes on a reel and has a sticky-backed tape that you peel off as it is applied. Most hardware and DIY stores stock it, as do larger glass merchants. It is usually used to stick onto windows to create an 'olde worlde' Tudor diamond-pane effect. There are several different widths and the reel usually comes with firmly onto the glass. It is more economic to buy the largest reel possible. Use a craft knife to cut lead accurately. Make sure you store lead in a dry place and keep it away from children as playing with lead can be dangerous. Always wash your hands thoroughly after using lead tape. It can be 'patinad' when the project is complete (see Patina overleaf).

This comes in a reel and is also sticky- **COPPER FOIL** together. It comes in different widths backed. It is used to edge the glass roundels so that you can attach a chain. The original function of using the copper tape or foil was to enable two pieces of glass to be joined together with solder without using the heavy lead came, especially useful when making more delicate pieces, such as lamps. This process was pioneered by Louis Comfort Tiffany. The foil was wrapped around the outside edges of the pieces of glass, then fluxed and soldered and the wider ones are very useful where two pieces of glass are fixed together. Melted solder is run around on the top of the copper foil to strengthen the tape and provide a good base for attaching the chain. This foil is available from stained-glass suppliers and craft catalogues. With wider foil you can create a decorative effect by using pinking shears to give an interesting scalloped border. This looks particularly good with dried-flower glass arrangements.

Solder is a mixture **SOLDER, FLUX AND SOLDERING IRONS** very quickly. If you of tin and lead and is used for fixing glass panels together and forming a solid border for single glass projects, such as roundels and sun catchers, Christmas angels, butterflies and window panels. It comes in a reel or in a stick. The recommended mix for solder is 50% lead and 50% tin, as this will not solidify too quickly when working. The plumber's solder will work, but it is not very flexible as it becomes hard get hot solder on your skin wash immediately with plenty of cold water, as it can easily burn.

Flux is a chemical used as a 'glue' to enable the solder to stick to the two surfaces. It is painted on to the lead or copper foil before the solder is applied. This can be bought in hardware stores, in stick or liquid form. Wash your hands thoroughly after using as it quite corrosive on the skin.

A soldering iron is used to melt the solder so that it can flow and coat the area that has been previously fluxed. When it is set it becomes firm very quickly, however it remains very hot, so be careful. The soldering iron can be electric or gas powered. Weller make an electric soldering iron for stained-glass work which has a thermostat and remains at a constant heat while working. It is important to be very careful using a soldering iron as they can cause severe burns. Always put the iron down on a stand or a brick, keep the cable well away from your body and turn the iron off immediately when you've finished working. Never let children or pets near the iron when it is hot, as it can be caught up easily and inflict severe burns. The lip is replaceable as it does wear out after a while.

PATINA

Patina is a fluid which is painted onto the solder to create several effects and to cover the new silvery finish of freshly applied solder. Patinas are supplied either by stained-glass suppliers or by mail order. Recently on the market is a new range of solder patina in two different finishes, opaque and transparent. The opaque comes in white, blue, green gold, red, and the transparent comes in brown, yellow, teal, green, black, red, blue and purple.

This versatile stain dries in minutes to a durable, fade-proof sheen, and is especially effective as a complimentary colour scheme. It is also available by mail order or contact the manufacturer (see Suppliers and Stockists) for your nearest stockist.

CHAINS AND RINGS

Chains for soldering onto roundels should be sturdy enough to hold the weight of the glass, and try to get a brass-based chain as it won't rust. You can pick up silver chains at jumble sales and junk shops and it's a good idea to build up a collection of chain for future projects. Most DIY stores sell chain by the metre or foot. Brass curtain rings and copper plumbing rings are ideal for creating hanging points, and take the soldering well. They are very cheap if you buy them at a hardware or DIY store.

p r a c t i c a l w o r k s h o p

If you want to create your own glass **CUTTING GLASS** cooking oil will do if you haven't blanks for panels and roundels, you will need to got any. The mail-order craft companies stock cut the glass. Most hardware stores stock cutters cutting oil as do stained-glass suppliers and most as do most glaziers. It is important when cutting glaziers. Glass cutters require a lot of practice to glass to have a sharp cutter and to use cutting use well, and I prefer to use a pistol grip cutter oil. I usually use lamp oil, but even a light available from most stained-glass suppliers.

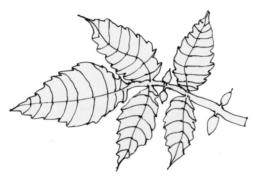

The design of a glass **CHOOSING THE RIGHT DESIGN** divide a blank piece of project is most important, because if the design paper (the same size as your glass) into the same is not right, the finished work will not have the number of squares. Enlarge or reduce (as maximum impact. If you can find a stained-glass appropriate) each small square of pattern onto window pattern book, available from stained- the blank piece of paper, until you have glass supplies shops or even from a library, you transferred the whole design. will see that the designs are usually quite simple If you are using your own design, and have in shape. This is because glass is difficult to cut access to a photocopier, you can make copies of and it is better to make pattern pieces easy to several images and arrange them together to cut and fix together. However, the same suit your needs. You could also trace off the principle applies to painted glass - the simpler designs and assemble the component parts to the design the more effective it will look. make a pattern. It can be helpful to go over the

If you are using a design from the pattern finished pattern with black felt-tip and to blank library in this book, simply place it under the out any superfluous lines with typing glass you are going to work on. You can enlarge correction fluid. When designing a roundel or a it or reduce it to fit your glass using a panel, don't position the pattern too close to photocopier or the grid method. For the grid the edge as it may be obscured by the foil method, divide the pattern up into squares and edging.

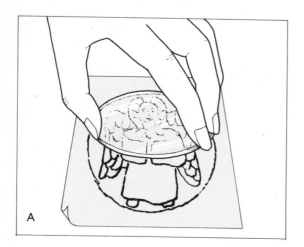

When you are sure that your **USING OUTLINER** design. For those who cannot design looks balanced, and fills the shape properly, place the glass over the pattern (Fig. A). Check that the glass is free from grease by using a spray glass cleaner. Take the outliner of your choice and try it out on scrap paper, just to make sure that it is running smoothly. Keep the nozzle clean at all times and remember to put the lid on when not using - it dries out in seconds. Carefully draw the design on top of the glass, tracing the pattern underneath (Fig. B). Start furthest away so that the lines are not smudged as you work. Don't be too elaborate, simple lines are the best. Keep clear and un-blobby by drawing firmly. It's a bit like drawing with toothpaste at first... squeeze and draw.

When you have finished, let it dry thoroughly, usually for about half an hour. It's a good idea to outline several pieces of glass at a time so that you have a selection of projects to work on. At this stage, when you hold up your glass it should reveal the outline of your design. For those who cannot draw, this is quite an encouraging moment, as the design usually looks competent and ready to work on. If your lines are coming out blobby, check the nozzle to see if there is any dried outliner stuck in the end. It is important that the outliner dries thoroughly before applying the paint, otherwise it will spread into the wet paint and make it look dirty.

When using outliner for a design on a bottle or jar, start at the top and gradually work down in a spiral movement. If you are copying a design through the glass, make sure that it is firmly taped on and doesn't come adrift and stick to the glass, your hand and the paint brush. Either tape the design on the inside of the jar (Fig. C) or on the opposite side of the bottle, so that the design can be seen through the bottle (Fig. D). When using the gold and silver outliner for top decoration on bottles or jars, make sure that the glass paint is dry before applying the outliner so that you get a really crisp finish.

C

D

GLASS PAINTING

When the outline is finished and dry, place the glass on a sheet of white paper so that the design lines show up clearly. Decide what colours you are going to use and where - the right colours will make or break the effect. Simple colours look good and the glow of light through the glass will draw the eye. Too many colours will jumble up the design, taking away the impact. If you are designing something that will feature in a northern light, colours like red, yellow and orange will warm up the light. Blue and green do well in southern light and in the east and the west you can use all the colours. However, you will be surprised at how much the light changes the colour values throughout the day.

Don't be mean with the paint, but use a cheap brush such as a child's paintbrush. Don't use a good watercolour one that holds paint; glass paint needs to run off the brush and onto the glass. Paint carefully inside the outliner, it's just like colouring-in at school! Most glass paints are quite viscous, they tend to run over the surface quite quickly, so make sure you contain the paint within the outliner. You can use masking tape to screen off areas that are not to be painted. Let each colour dry for about twenty minutes before painting a different one next to it. The paint will take about twelve hours to dry completely.

Work carefully, cleaning your brushes between colours. Leave to dry in a dust-free and cat-free zone. (One of our cats went to sleep on a freshly painted roundel and had to be cut free. The flowers didn't look so glorious either, with a liberal layer of black and white fur.)

CREATING A BORDER FOR ROUNDELS

When making roundels, you will need to create a border around the glass on which to attach the chain. Take the copper tape and begin to peel off the backing tape. Place the glass edge in the centre of the foil strip and wrap around the rim (Fig. A). Using a flat tool such as a wooden spoon or a lambrequin (available from stained glass suppliers), flatten the foil down on both sides and the outside edge, making sure that the foil is firmly attached to the glass (Fig. B).

Heat up the soldering iron and, meanwhile, prepare the surface of copper foil by brushing on flux. When the soldering iron is hot, take the solder in one hand and the iron in the other. Touch the soldering iron to the end of the solder until it melts. Drop a bead of solder onto the copper foil. It should make a hissing sound indicating that it has flux underneath it. If it doesn't hiss, put some flux on the foil or joint, otherwise the solder will not stick. Place the soldering iron on the solder and gently move along, within the pool of melted solder (Fig. C). Do not drag the solder as it will go lumpy.

If the solder gets too thick, take the soldering iron and carefully go round the foil again, slowly letting the solder smooth out under the tip of the iron. The excess will fall off in a little ball which you can leave to cool and keep in a pot for re-using. As the solder cools, it will set with a silvery appearance.

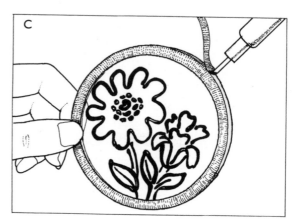

FIXING A CHAIN TO A ROUNDEL

Cut the chain to size and solder each end on to the sides of the roundel, quite near the top, so that the roundel hangs with the design correctly positioned.

APPLYING STICK-ON LEAD

If you want to create a really heavy lead effect, you'll need to use stick-on lead rather than outliner. Unroll the lead tape and use sharp scissors to cut the tape to the required length. Unpeel the backing and stick the tape down along the lines of the design. Smooth the lead tape down on the glass using the small plastic tool usually supplied with the tape for this purpose (Fig. D). Where lead lines cross each other, take a blunt knife edge and press down on either side of the intersection to create a square raised section (Fig. E). Try to run the tape in long fluid lines, avoiding too many cuts. Keep the joins neat by cutting the tape at matching angles (Fig. F).

For an added effect, add blobs of solder to the lead junctions. Just brush with flux and gently add a touch of solder so that it forms a melted cross effect. Allow to cool, turn the work over and solder the other side. Clean well with glass cleaner when cooled. Solder gets very hot and can burn skin, so it is important not to handle items until cool.

Wash your hands thoroughly after soldering to remove lead and flux.

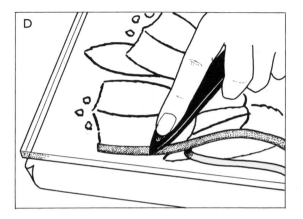

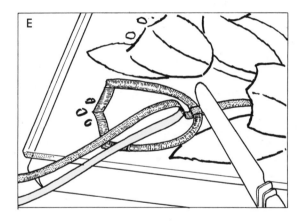

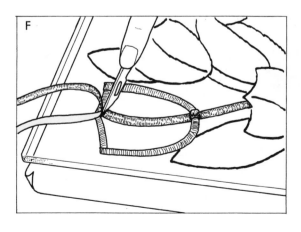

To achieve an antique effect, brush **APPLYING PATINA** To obtain coppery patina, it is on a patina which will darken the solder. When possible to mix up copper sulphate (from the dry, clean with glass cleaner. There are several chemist) and water and paint it on. After the colours, including black, silver, copper and solder has darkened, polish with metal polish to antiqued, which can be used for different effects. bring out a coppery tone on the solder.

SUPPLIERS AND STOCKISTS

Glass is best obtained from your local glass merchants. They will cut the glass to size and grind the edges if required. Look for a glazier who is a member of the Glass and Glazing Federation, as they will have all the current regulations concerning glass and can tell you what you need for any specific project. Most good art and craft shops carry glass paints, outliner and many of the other items needed for painting on glass. However, the following companies will supply various products by mail order, to anywhere in the world.

Panduro Hobby
Westway House, Transport Avenue
Brentford, Middlesex TW8 9HF
Phone: 01392 427788

To order goods from Panduro you must first buy their catalogue. This is available at W. H. Smiths (£4.50) or direct from Panduro (£4.95). They require a minimum order value of £2.00 excluding carriage and can supply the following items: glass paints, thinner, glass and acrylic blanks and ready-chained roundels.

Fred Aldous Ltd
PO Box 135, 37 Lever Street
Manchester M60 1UX
Phone: 0161 236 2477
Fax: 0161 236 6075

To order goods from Fred Aldous Ltd please send two first-class stamps for a catalogue. They require a minimum order value of £2.00 excluding carriage and can supply the following items: glass (personal callers only), glass paints, stick-on lead, copper foil tape, soldering irons, flux solder, patina, carbon paper, glass cleaner, and ready-chained roundels.

SPECIAL OFFER FOR
UK READERS

PEBEO Glass Painting Set from Philip and Tacey Mail Order. If you would like to order a starter kit, normally worth £19.99, containing the following items:

• 4 x 45ml bottles of Vitrail Glass Paint
• 1 x 45ml bottle of thinner
• 1 x brush
• 1 x 20 ml tube of outliner
• 1 glass bottle to paint

please send a cheque for £11.95 plus £2.50 postage and packing made payable to Philip and Tacey Ltd, and quoting ref P754.004, to:

Philip and Tacey Ltd
Department 9604
North Way, Andover
Hants, SP10 5BA

Credit card orders can be accepted by telephone. Please call 01264 332171.

NOTE: This offer is valid only for orders received by July 1st 1997. After that date readers should contact Philip and Tacey to check the price and availability.

READERS IN AUSTRALIA AND
NEW ZEALAND

The following retails outlets stock a range of products used in glass painting. They are open to personal shoppers and also supply by mail order. Please phone or fax for further details.

Australia

Rough Sketch
469-473 Glenhuntly Road
ELSTERNWICK VIC 3185
Phone: 03 9523 8894
Fax: 03 9528 3508

Lugarno Craft Cottage
243 Belmore Road
RIVERWOOD NSW 2210
Phone: 02 584 1944
Fax: 02 533 1485

Art Land Indooroopilly
Unit 7
Indooroopilly Central
272 Moggil Road
INDOOROOPILLY QLD 4068
Phone: 07 3878 5536
Fax: 07 3878 9464

New Zealand

Auckland Folk Art Centre
591 Remuera Road
Upland Village Remuera
AUCKLAND
Phone: 09 524 2936
Fax: 09 524 2649

Handcraft Supplies NZ (Ltd)
13-19 Rosebank Road
Avondale
AUCKLAND
Phone: 09 828 9834
Fax: 09 828 3636

Section 1

PAINTED

PANELS

Vibrant Poppy
r o u n d e l

THE poppy, so simple, so beautiful, is one of the most popular subjects for stained-glass projects. The vibrant crimson petals and flowery shapes are stunning viewed with light shining through the glass. To create this design, either use the poppy pattern in the pattern library section of this book or look through some gardening catalogues and greeting cards for references. Try to get a flower arrangement that includes flowers and buds. For background you can include grasses and corn, as they grow naturally with poppies in the wild.

Poppies don't have to be restricted to roundels, they look fabulous on mirrors and plates and quite stunning when painted onto a glass jug. Poppies stencilled around a window with cornflowers and wisps of corn liven up a dark corner, and painted poppies on a glass lamp-shade produce a mysterious oriental effect.

This project is photographed on p104

MATERIALS

poppy design from
pattern library
(page 113)

1 x 15cm (6 in)
glass roundel, float
or Flemish glass

black outliner

glass paints

copper foil

solder and flux

chain

patina (optional)

glass cleaner

soldering iron

T O   M A K E

1

Select the poppy design, place the glass over the pattern, centering it to make a balanced image. With the black outliner trace carefully over the pattern. Make sure that the flowers and leaves form a harmonious grouping within the roundel. Do not draw the design too close to the rim as it will be covered by the foil edging. Work from top to bottom to avoid smudges. Leave to dry for 30 minutes.

2

Place the roundel on top of some white paper, outliner-side up, and paint the design carefully with glass paints, making sure to take the paint up to the outliner. Add some yellow to the leaves to give a natural mottled effect. Clean your brushes between colours using turps or white spirit. Leave to dry for about 12 hours.

3

To finish the roundel, wrap the outer edge of the glass with copper foil, making sure it is firmly pressed down. Heat up the soldering iron, paint on flux, and solder around both sides and the outside edge to form a silvery metal frame. Paint on patina if required – the antique copper finish looks good with this project.

4

Cut the chain to size and solder onto the sides of the roundel. Clean well with glass cleaner and hang in a window using a sturdy hook.

Please refer to The Practical Workshop for full instructions on each technique.

Jewelled Peacock
r o u n d e l

PAINTED PANELS

THE magnificent peacock, mysterious denizen of exotic gardens, is a really popular subject for a window roundel. With or without added jewels, this produces a stunning effect that will brighten up any window. The strong blues, greens and turquoises of the plumage look terrific against greenery and are particularly spectacular when used in conservatory windows. Another room that would look wonderful with a peacock roundel is a bathroom, especially when teamed with toning paint and accessories. The pattern library gives a couple of different designs and, for further reference, try bird books or William Morris wallpaper. You can even use your own photographs, photocopied and enlarged. For accurate colour reference, buy a peacock feather from a florist or craft shop.

This project is photographed on p104

M A T E R I A L S

peacock design from pattern library (page 113)

30cm (12 in) glass roundel, float or Flemish glass

black outliner

flat-bottomed glass

jewels

glass glue

glass paints

copper foil

solder and flux

chain

patina (optional)

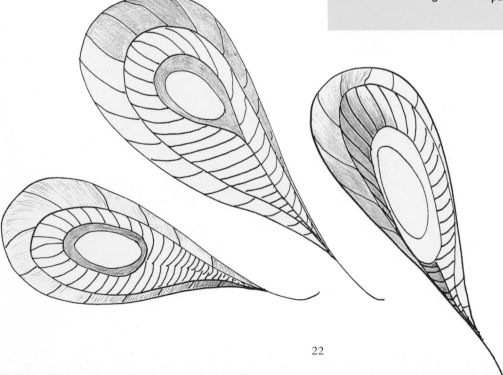

22

TO MAKE

1

Using the peacock pattern, enlarge it to fit the roundel. Place the glass over the pattern and, using the outliner, draw the peacock onto the glass. Leave it to dry in a dust-free area.

2

Place the roundel on white paper, look carefully at the peacock and if you are planning on using jewels, now is the time to glue them onto the eye parts of the feathers. Follow the glass glue instructions carefully. Then paint in the rest of the peacock and leave to dry. Hold it up to the light when it is dry to check that all parts are covered properly with glass paint. Touch up the painting and leave to dry for 24 hours.

3

Wrap the copper foil around the edges, making sure that the foil is firmly stuck down. Paint the foil with flux and solder around the edges. Cut the chain to size, then flux and solder the chain onto the roundel. Make sure you use enough solder as a glass roundel is quite heavy and needs to be firmly attached. Paint on patina, if required.

4

Clean the roundel and hang in a window or conservatory. These roundels look extra special if you tie complementary ribbons to the points where the chain is soldered onto the roundel.

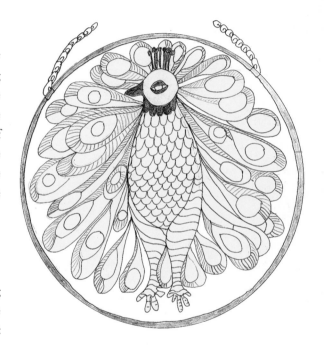

Please refer to The Practical Workshop for full instructions on each technique.

Blackberry Cottage
roundel

THIS is a charming and novel way of displaying the name of your house, with the additional benefit that, because it is displayed inside the house, it is safe from light-fingered collectors! Plus, it will also be visible at night, with the lights of the house shining through the

blackberries. The house sign can be displayed in a window or perhaps above a door if you have a fanlight.

Last year I created a large roundel for an arts and tea shop in America, featuring a large teapot wreathed with flowers and the shop's logo. All manner of ideas and themes can be used and a house-name roundel makes a wonderful house-warming present. Other ideas for house roundels might be to incorporate the family name as well as the house name or even the street name and number. House roundels or panels can be framed in wood and suspended from hooks for extra strength.

This project is photographed on p88

MATERIALS

blackberry design from pattern library (page 114)

lettering cut from magazines or newspapers

glass roundel (any size)

black outliner

glass paint

copper foil

solder and flux

chain

patina (optional)

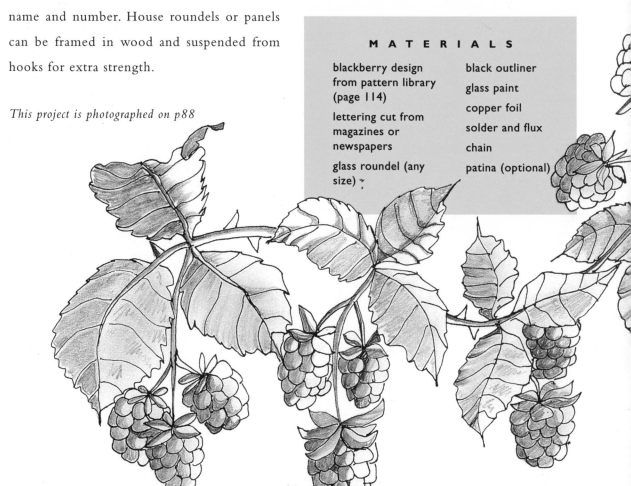

T O   M A K E

1

Select the blackberry design, copy it, and then draw out your chosen lettering. Cut up the copy of the blackberry pattern and arrange the berries and leaves around your lettering. Place the glass over the layout and trace over the design with outliner.

2

When the outliner is dry (about 30 minutes), carefully paint in the design. In this case, you will need blue, purple, brown and green for the blackberries. The lettering is picked out in a berry red to give some definition. If you wish, you can pick out the little spiky bits of the blackberry sepals and also some of the individual blackberry fruits with gold outliner.

 3

When the paint is dry, carefully wrap the foil around the edges, paint on flux and solder the rim on both sides and the edge. Cut the chain to fit, and solder firmly onto the roundel. Paint with patina if required.

4

Clean the roundel and hang in position. Remember to hang it so it can be read from the outside!

> **TIP**
>
> If you are not confident about doing your own lettering, here is an easy way to get round the problem. Find some magazines with large lettering on the pages. Cut out a selection of letters and keep them in a folder for re-use. Pick out enough letters to spell out the required name and arrange them on a sheet of white paper the same size as your roundel.

Please refer to The Practical Workshop for full instructions on each technique.

M*onet's* waterlilies panel

PAINTED
PANELS

THIS is a freehand interpretation of the well-loved impressionist painting of lilies floating in a pond, which I first did as a bathroom window to be installed in a double-glazed unit. The glass paint is allowed to flow and stream and diffuse so that a wonderful watery effect is achieved.

The secret of this technique is to be very relaxed and not worry too much how the paint goes on. The whole effect will take place in front of your eyes and if it doesn't look right, you can rub it off with a cloth quite easily before it dries. This technique works well for windows that need to let in the light but still give privacy. However it may be prudent to use a blind at night, as an electric light would shine very clearly through Monet's waterlilies!

This project is photographed on p89

MATERIALS

waterlily panel
photograph for
reference (page 89)

30cm x 60cm
(12in x 24in) panel,
float or Flemish glass
(or cut to fit window)

blue felt-tip pen

glass paints

gold outliner

TO MAKE

Lightly draw in water lines and outlines of waterlilies with blue felt-tip pen. Mix paints separately using clear glass paint or medium shades of watery glass colours.

Paint liberally and quickly in horizontal lines, letting the colours mingle and swirl together, then take a brush loaded with water, or turps, and carefully flick on droplets over the panel. Let them spread out and diffuse into the colours. It is advisable to put down plenty of newspaper for this project as it can get quite messy. When the whole panel is covered, carefully dab, with clean rag or kitchen roll, the areas where the lilies are to be painted in. Let it dry completely before tackling the next step.

3

Paint the lily pads in different shades of green. When they are dry, paint in the lilies in white, pink and yellow. Accent the stamens with gold outliner, and allow to dry thoroughly. If the panel is to go in a window, make sure that all the painting has been done right up to the edge before it is installed, to avoid touch-ups.

4

You can foil or solder the panel and hang it with a chain or place it in a wooden frame. Old picture frames complete with plain glass make ideal glass panels. The frames can be painted to match and decorated with dried flowers and shells, especially in pink and yellow tones.

Please refer to The Practical Workshop for full instructions on each technique.

Monet's garden roundel

The famous Bonchurch Pond lies outside my house, with all the magical colours and qualities of the English countryside. Nestled like a long mirror beneath the famous cliffs of the landslip, the pond reflects the colours of the sky amid the myriad hues of the surrounding plants and flowers - an ever changing palette of pinks, blues and shimmering aquamarine. This is all very reminiscent of Giverny, Monet's home in France, and this connection gave me the idea of creating a 'Monet' roundel.

This project is photographed on p109

PAINTED PANELS

MATERIALS

Monet's garden design from pattern library (page 115)

roundel (any size), Flemish glass preferred

black and gold outliner

glass paints

copper foil

solder and flux

chain

blue felt-tip pen

TO MAKE

1

Select the Monet's garden pattern and enlarge or reduce on a photocopier to suit the size of your roundel.

2

Place the glass roundel over the pattern and trace the bridge and the other strong lines with outliner. Lightly draw over the major parts of the rest of the design with the blue felt-tip pen.

3

Select the colours for the roundel, and carefully paint them in letting the colours bleed into each other. If you have some clear glass paint, drop some on in blobs over the roundel. The clear blobs will create a watery effect.

4

Carefully dab off the paint in the areas where the waterlilies will be (kitchen roll is good for this). When dry, paint in the lilies.

5

When the lilies are dry, carefully wrap the foil around the edges, paint on a flux and solder the rim on both sides and the edge. Cut the chain to fit, and solder firmly onto the roundel.

6

Clean the roundel and highlight the waterlilies with gold outliner. Hang in position.

Pressed Leaves
r o u n d e l

ONE of nature's spectacular free shows is the autumn leaf display. Outside my studio window hangs a cascade of glorious red, orange, peach, yellow and cinnamon Virginia creeper leaves. It is one of the great pleasures in life to go out on a September morning after the morning dew has dried off and collect leaves. These can then be dried between paper, or by placing them in a microwave oven, between blotting paper and weighed down with a brick.

PAINTED
PANELS

When creating a leaf roundel, use any autumn words that spring to mind, and write them round and round towards the centre of the arrangement. You could also create a Harvest Home Roundel with leaves, dried grasses and finely sliced seed cases.

This project is photographed on p84

MATERIALS

2 thin roundels, float glass preferred	copper foil
	solder and flux
selection of coloured autumn leaves	chain
	clear tape
gold outliner	

T O   M A K E

Arrange the leaves on top of a glass roundel. Try to ensure that they are arranged in a swirling movement and do not overlap too much as that would detract from the effect of the colours and shapes when viewed through the glass.

2

Carefully place the second roundel on top and tack to the first roundel with small pieces of clear tape. (These can be trimmed after soldering.)

Firmly tape the two pieces of glass together with the copper foil. Flux and solder and attach the chain. Trim off any excess tape and clean thoroughly.

4

Using the gold outliner, carefully write your chosen words around the outer rim of the roundel, working towards the centre.

Please refer to The Practical Workshop for full instructions on each technique.

Field Mice
r o u n d e l

DRIED grasses are stunning when viewed through glass, with every wispy blade and grain delineated, and the addition of field mice at play among the stalks adds a magical country feeling. If you look carefully there is a little corn fairy, hiding in the stalks watching them.

If you don't live near places where you can find grasses, dried flower suppliers or florists usually have a good supply. These are quite often dyed, so even more interesting pictures can be crafted.

Make sure to use flat grasses so that the two roundels can fit closely, when being foiled together.

M A T E R I A L S

field mice design
and fairy design
from pattern library
(page 115)

2 x 2mm thick glass
roundels, any size

compass

felt-tip pen

glass paint

outliner

a selection of
wild grasses

sticky tape

copper foil

solder and flux

chain

This project is photographed on p105

T O   M A K E

Decide on the colour for the border; if you are using coloured grasses they can be co-ordinated. Using a compass and a felt-tip pen, mark a 4cm (1.5in) wide border on each roundel, paint and put aside to dry.

Select the field mice pattern and fairy pattern and arrange in the centre of one roundel. Draw on the design with outliner and leave to dry.

Place the other roundel paint-side down, and arrange grasses in the centre.

**Please refer to The Practical Workshop for full
instructions on each technique.**

Put the roundel with the mice and fairy outline, paint-side up, on top of the roundel with grasses. Secure the two roundels together with clear tape. (This can be trimmed off after foiling.)

Clean the surface of the glass and carefully paint in the field mice and the fairy. Leave to dry.

Measure off the correct length of chain needed to hang the roundel and solder in place.

Firmly tape the roundels together with copper foil. Brush with flux and solder round.

Jolly Sailor
s i g n

PAINTED glass is an ideal medium for creating original and high-impact advertising signs. These signs can be made economically and changed when necessary. They can be hung in the window and suspended from hanging bars, displayed above doors or even used internally, in front of a mirror to reflect the light. It is a good idea to keep to really simple designs and a small range of eye-catching colours. This Jolly Sailor sign was designed for an outlet for yachting and boating clothing.

A pub sign is another ideal design project for painted glass as the light will shine through during the day, and it can be lit at night to attract attention. However, a few coats of varnish will be necessary if the sign is to be used outside.

This project is photographed on p94

M A T E R I A L S

jolly sailor design from pattern library (page 116)

sheet of suitable sized glass for this project

black outliner

glass paints

varnish (if used outside)

copper foil

solder

chain or rope hangings

T O   M A K E

Size and arrange the jolly sailor pattern to fit your piece of glass. Place the glass over the design and trace with the outliner.

Allow to dry and then paint carefully with the glass paints. To make it extra eye-catching you may need to paint two layers of paint to achieve a deeper colour. If the sign is to hang outside, it is wise to varnish it with polyurethane varnish for extra protection. (For this project I would use Malibu or Deka glass paints, if you can get them, as they are especially hardwearing.)

When the paint is dry, insert in frame or foil and solder the outside and attach a chain or rope for hanging.

TIP

An empty picture frame, complete with glass, will make an instant hanging sign, with a couple of eye hooks attached to the top. As this is a nautical theme, the sign would look very authentic suspended from rope hangers.

Please refer to The Practical Workshop for full instructions on each technique.

Jungle Scene
panel

ONE of the most interesting commissions that I have been asked to do was to disguise a terrible mistake created when a local hotelier had an extension built to the dining room. It wasn't until you sat down at the table that you realised that the view from the new windows was hideous.

PAINTED
PANELS

My task was to design a tropical window, very dense at the bottom and fading out towards the top, to camouflage the dismal scene. I used Flemish glass to further obscure the horrible sight and, armed with a collection of plant photocopies from a gardening magazine, I set to work. By moving all the plant pictures round and round under the glass, I was able to create a very dense foliage area at the base of the window. The colours at the base were dark and rich and progressed to colourful flowers and stalks as they moved up the window. There were toucans, parrots and butterflies, but no monkeys, natives with spears or crocodiles to put the diners off their meal.

This project is photographed on p83

MATERIALS

sheet of Flemish glass, cut to size of window

designs and photocopies of tropical foliage, plants and animals or design from

pattern library (page 117)

black outliner

glass paints

TO MAKE

1

Draw out the design on a large piece of paper the same size as your pane of glass. Move the drawings around to fill the entire space at the base of the design, getting sparser towards the top of the window. Butterflies look very good at the top of the window; try to place them so it looks as if they are in flight.

2

Place the design under the glass and draw over with black outliner, starting at the top and working down. Allow to dry.

3

Paint carefully with glass paints, again working from the top of the panel down to avoid smudges. Allow to dry completely.

4

Clean with glass cleaner, and touch up any areas that have escaped the brush. Install in the window frame, painted side inside.

Please refer to The Practical Workshop for full instructions on each technique.

THE CRAFT OF
painting on
GLASS

Section 2

IDEAS FOR

THE HOME

Floral
door panel

THIS design for a glass front-door panel is based on a free style, rambling California poppy, so that it can be repeated depending on the size of your panel. There is no need to remove the existing door panel. Have a glass panel cut to fit the aperture of the existing panel and, when the new panel has been painted, and cleaned, run a bead of glass glue around the edge of the existing panel. Carefully press the newly painted panel of glass on top, glass-painted side inward, and wait until it has bonded. You can run a rebate round if the door panel is seated in deeply or if your new panel is fractionally too small. Because this design is painted all over, be sure to check that there are no gaps in the paintwork before fixing it into the door.

This project is photographed on p100

MATERIALS

California poppy design from the pattern library (page 116)

glass door panel cut to fit the existing aperture

black outliner

glass paints

stick-on lead

clear glass varnish or polyurethane varnish

TO MAKE

1

Draw out the design for the California poppy to fit your door panel. Place the glass over the design and draw over it with black outliner.

2

When the outliner is dry, paint in the flowers and background with glass paints.

3

Select the main stem areas and top lead with stick-on lead tape. (See The Practical Workshop section for full instructions.)

4

Clean the existing door panel and clean and varnish the new one. In bright sunlight, glue the new panel in place and wait until it is firmly bonded.

Tulip window panel

GLOWING tulips entwined within a leaded border make a classic stained-glass window design. Tulips are a very popular subject for stained glass, as they are a relatively simple shape and come in dense, glowing colours. This design features a few simple tulips, but more intricate tulip designs can be seen in many William Morris wallpapers and fabrics. This method of glass painting and top leading with stick-on lead, produces a highly traditional stained-glass effect. If solder is applied to the joints with a solid blob effect, the impression of a genuine leaded window appears even more realistic.

This project is photographed on p93

IDEAS FOR THE HOME

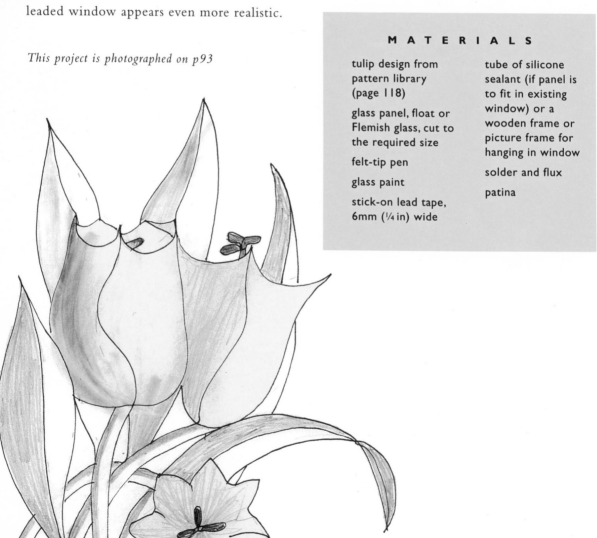

MATERIALS

tulip design from pattern library (page 118)

glass panel, float or Flemish glass, cut to the required size

felt-tip pen

glass paint

stick-on lead tape, 6mm (¼ in) wide

tube of silicone sealant (if panel is to fit in existing window) or a wooden frame or picture frame for hanging in window

solder and flux

patina

T O   M A K E

Select the tulip pattern and enlarge or reduce to fit your panel. Place the glass over the pattern and draw the design with a felt-tip pen. (If the window is in a position where extra privacy is required, use Flemish glass. For extra security use laminated or toughened glass.)

Paint tulips, leaves and background and allow to dry thoroughly.

Unroll the lead tape, and use a craft knife or sharp scissors to cut the tape to correct lengths. Stick down over the felt-tip lines, trying to keep the joins neat by cutting at angles. Make sure the tape is well smoothed down on the glass.

Turn over the panel and repeat the taped on lead, making sure that the lead lines match up with the ones on the front. It is important to tape both sides of the panel to achieve a proper leaded effect.

Clean finished panel and glue over existing window as described on page 37. Alteratively, frame as required and hang.

Please refer to The Practical Workshop for full instructions on each technique.

Dragon
door panel

GOTHIC designs, incorporating acanthus leaves, fleur de lys, stylised flowers and dragons, were especially loved by the Pre-Raphaelites and used in designs for glass, wallpaper and textiles. Although the method of construction for this panel is not significantly different from the tulip panel, greater care must be taken in drawing out the pattern and in selecting the right colours. Because it is more complicated, the colours must be right and not filled in randomly. I have found it useful to trace the design onto a sheet of plain paper and do a trial colour version. Tape it over the door panel area for a couple of days and see what effect there is at different times of the day and what happens to wallpaper and walls when colours are directed on them. Glass jewels look absolutely splendid incorporated into this kind of design. The centre of the flowers and the eye of the dragon flash and shine when the door is moved and at night the rich glow of colours and jewels spills out into the night.

This project is photographed on p103

MATERIALS

dragon door design from pattern library (page 119)

door panel in 6mm (¼ in) float or Flemish glass

sheet of paper the same size as your door panel

felt-tip pen

black outliner

glass paints

glass jewels

glass glue

stick-on lead

polyurethane or clear glass varnish

TO MAKE

Draw out the design to fit your glass panel on a sheet of paper. You may find that the grid method works well here. Divide up the blank sheet of paper into sixteenths and do the same with the dragon pattern. Copy each small square of the pattern onto the blank sheet, square by square, until the entire pattern appears. Colour in a copy of this, using a felt-tip pen, for your practice colour version.

When the pattern is completed, lay the glass carefully over it and draw on the outliner.

3.

Allow to dry thoroughly and, working from the top, carefully paint with glass paints. Leave the areas for the glass jewels unpainted because glass glue does not stick to paint.

4

Glue the glass jewels in position. Stick the lead strips in place, referring to The Practical Workshop section.

TIP

Choose laminated glass or toughened glass for an exterior door. Check with a Glass and Glazing Federation glazier when ordering the glass.

5

When finished, clean thoroughly and paint on a thin layer of varnish. Install in the door with the painted side on the inside, as described on page 37.

Please refer to The Practical Workshop for full instructions on each technique.

Conservatory
creations

IDEAS FOR
THE HOME

A few years ago we built a large conservatory extension to our house which was a monument of economy and inspirational design. There were of course large expanses of glass that needed to be decorated and embellished. The first thing that I did was to create a painted floral frieze that ran all round the conservatory above the windows. I had thought of making a straightforward leaded glass set of panels, but it would have looked too heavy.

The next areas that needed some attention were the large triangular spaces at either end of the building. In order to provide privacy in winter when the trees are bare, I created a jungle of flowers, birds and butterflies, some rabbits and a cat. I have enjoyed this scene for the past few years and next year I am going to scrape it all off with a window scraper and paint a beach scene with mountains, forests, surfers and California beach flowers.

Another interesting way to use glass painting is to create greenery which reduces the glare of the sun without the expense of conservatory blinds. You can of course include birds and flowers in the greenery to create an exotic effect.

This project is photographed on p106

This project is photographed on p106

MATERIALS

patterns for flowers, birds, cats, greenery etc.	glass paints
	masking tape
white paper	painting rag or kitchen roll
felt-tip pens	
black outliner	polyurethane matt varnish

TO MAKE

1

For smaller panels, select the design you want to use on the glass and transfer it to plain white paper. Cut out paper to fit the glass panel.

Tape the design with masking tape onto the exterior of the glass, as the glass-painted side must face inward. Draw on the design with a felt-tip pen, remove the paper and redraw with black outliner.

TIP

When creating large pieces of shading greenery, do one branch at a time so that you can see how much more is needed. You can glue glass jewels on unpainted areas for a shining berry effect, but this will have to be done in the daylight for the glass glue to work properly.

2

When the outliner is dry, paint the panel with the glass paint. Start at the top and use only a little paint on the brush. Work with a rag or kitchen roll handy to catch any drips before they set. For larger expanses of conservatory window, work on one panel at a time so that you don't have too much wet, sticky paint on the go at once.

To avoid any damage by damp, such as condensation, it is a good idea to varnish the windows with polyurethane matt varnish.

Please refer to The Practical Workshop for full instructions on each technique.

Fruit and Flowers
mirror garland

THE natural progression for a dedicated glass painter is to move from painting on clear glass to painting on mirror glass. The effect of glass paint colours reflected in and out of the design gives a completely different dimension to the project. You can get mirror glass cut to size at the glaziers and many shops sell plain mirrors very cheaply. You can also use mirror tiles which come in several different sizes and finishes. The smoky bronze ones look great with white or pastel glass paints, high-lighted with gold or silver outliner.

One of my favourite designs for softening the lines of a plain square-topped mirror is to paint a wonderful garland, swagged across the top and trailing down the sides. This can be fruit or flowers or even exotic greenery with glass 'jewelled' berries peeping out amid the leaves.

This project is photographed on p95

IDEAS FOR THE HOME

MATERIALS

fruit and flowers design from pattern library (page 120) or a selection of your own designs

plain white paper

tracing paper

sharp pencil

plain mirror, framed or unframed

felt-tip pen

black outliner

glass paints (or spray-on car paints)

glass jewels

glass glue

newsprint

glass cleaner

masking tape

Please refer to The Practical Workshop for full instructions on each technique.

TO MAKE

Method 1 – carbon paper

1

Select the fruit and flowers design from the pattern library or create your own design for the garland. For a fine assortment of flowers and leaves, trace off shapes from chintz curtain material or flowery wallpaper onto a large piece of plain white paper. Cut out a selection of flowers and leaves and arrange them into the garland shape.

2

Working with the mirror horizontal, thoroughly clean the surface of the mirror, using spray-on glass cleaner. Carefully draw the garland pattern onto sheets of tracing paper, taped together to get the size needed. Decide where the garland is going to be, making sure that the design is centred, and that there are equal amounts of flowers and foliage on each side.

3

Place some carbon paper, ink-side down, on the mirror. Place the tracing paper over the carbon and transfer the garland design on to the surface of the mirror. Lightly go over the design with felt-tip pen to make it clearer to follow.

4

Draw over design with the outliner, leave to dry and then gently wipe off the felt-tip lines. The design should now be outlined on glass and ready to paint. Look at the design at this point and decide whether it needs more leaves or flowers.

5

When you are satisfied with the overall appearance of the design, paint with glass paints and leave to dry. Make sure that the paint goes right up to the outline, as the mirror will emphasize any gaps. (Do not paint any areas where you will be applying glass jewels, as glass glue will not stick to paint.)

6

If you are intending to use glass jewels on your project, now is the time to glue them on.

7

When dry, inspect your project, check to see if there is sufficient coverage of the glass paint, and touch up any missed parts. Clean the glass again to remove any finger prints. Hang the mirror on the wall, in a position where light will glance across it to reveal the hidden colours and shimmers of your design.

TIP

If your mirror is fixed to the wall and cannot be worked on the flat, use a stencil (see overleaf) and work with car-spray paint. (You cannot use glass paint because it is too runny and will seep under the edges.)

T O   M A K E   continued

Using stencils is a little more complicated and you cannot paint the glass paint directly through the stencil, because it is too runny and will seep under the edges.

Method 2
– stencilling the outline

To make a stencil, take some stencil card, available from craft shops and by mail order, and transfer the design from the tracing paper onto the card. Using a very sharp craft knife, cut out the petal and leaf shapes and the major connecting stems to create your own customized stencil.

Tape the stencil into position on the mirror and using the felt-tip pen draw round the inside edge of the stencil to transfer the design onto the mirror. If you are repeating the same stencil, move to the next position and retape.

3

Then using the outliner, clarify the design and, when dry, remove the felt-tip pen lines. Follow Method 1 from step 5 onwards.

Please refer to The Practical Workshop for full instructions on each technique.

Method 3
– stencilling the whole design

1

Follow Method 2 to make the stencil, tape it onto the mirror and gently spray on the car paint. Hold the can at least 30cm (12in) away. If you want a really diffused effect, try spraying through an empty cardboard toilet roll cut in half (longways). Do this in a well-ventilated room as the fumes of this paint can be quite heavy. Use lots of newspaper and have plenty of white spirit on hand to clean up.

Remove the stencil after twenty minutes to allow time to dry off, move to the next position and retape.

TIP

If you want to achieve an etched glass effect, then using stencils with white glass paint or white car-spray paint works really well. Try to get a slightly uneven effect as this adds to the authenticity.

Daffodil lamp

OLD-fashioned oil lamps used to have glass chimneys that slotted in around the wick to carry the fumes of the oil or gas away from the immediate area. Nowadays many electric imitation oil lamps are made on the same principle and have removable glass chimneys.

These lamps are available at hardware stores and specialist lighting shops. If you don't have one you can improvise with a glass chimney popped over a nightlight on a terracotta flowerpot saucer. You can use any of the traditional designs, but the nature of the shape allows some fun experimenting. My daughter, Natasha, created a terrific patchwork painted chimney with the stitching indicated in gold outliner. Use with scented candles to add to the pleasure. This daffodil pattern is bright and fresh and looks delightful in a kitchen or dining room.

This project is photographed on p91

MATERIALS

daffodil design
from pattern library
(page 121)

plain glass chimney
lamp

black outliner

glass paints

clear glass paint
or polyurethane
varnish

TO MAKE

1

Trace the daffodil design, and tape it to the inside of the glass chimney. Draw on the design with the black outliner.

2

When the outliner is dry, paint in the daffodils in strong clear colours. As the light source is so close to the glass, a second coat of paint gives greater depth.

3

When the paint is dry, finish with a coat of clear glass paint or polyurethane varnish.

Please refer to
The Practical Workshop
for full instructions on
each technique.

Mock Cranberry
glass

CRANBERRY glass is named after the delicious red colour of the glass. It is immensely collectible and beginning to be quite expensive. I devised this technique because I had a collection of cranberry glass but none of the sets was complete. I needed some matching dessert

plates, but I only had plain glass ones which didn't add much to the festive scene. Inspiration… out with the glass paints and *voila!* – cranberry dessert plates. Naturally after this success several more plain glass items were magically transformed into cranberry glass. An added bonus is that they look absolutely fabulous in a display cabinet or perched on a window frame. So much so that an antique dealer banged on the door to see if I would sell them! Clear glass dishes are very cheap and can be found in lots of stores. Once painted, these dishes can be washed in cool water or cleaned with glass cleaner but are not dishwasher safe.

This project is photographed on p96

MATERIALS

plain glass plate

red and blue glass paint (or cranberry-

coloured if you can find it)

gold outliner

TO MAKE

1

Mix up glass paint to the approximate shade of cranberry glass if you are trying to match an existing set.

2

Evenly paint the underside of a plain glass plate (or whatever you wish to transform) and allow to dry.

3

If you like, add a gold edge to the rim or gold spots all over using the gold outliner.

TIP

If you are painting a bowl, turn it upside down and paint from the top in a spiral direction.

Please refer to The Practical Workshop for full instructions on each technique.

Butterfly dome

IDEAS FOR
THE HOME

LURKING in the back of my kitchen cupboards were two glass cheese domes that I had been presented with long ago and promptly forgotten about. In my house, lumps of cheese tend to be devoured long before any cheese dome can be utilised however, for a dinner party, I do like to serve a selection of cheeses. The average cheese dome is not very exciting, but guests at my house would surely expect me to produce something unusual. I painted little mice all over the first dome, and had them peeking out from poppies and cornstalks.

For the second one (featured here) I used a theme of butterflies and worked with shiny opalescent foil wrapping paper, dusted with glitter powder.

This project is photographed on p110

MATERIALS

butterfly design from pattern library (page 122)

glass cheese dome

black, silver and gold outliner

clear glass paint or polyurethane varnish

glitter powder

small pieces of opalescent foil wrapping paper

glass paints

tracing paper

TO MAKE

1
Trace and cut out the butterfly design, and tape to the inside of the dome. Draw on as many butterflies as you wish with black outliner.

2
Paint over parts of the dome with clear glass paint or polyurethane varnish. While it is still tacky, scatter silver glitter in thin trails. Then, cut the opalescent foil into tiny pieces and scatter over the sticky areas of the glass dome.

3
When the varnish is dry, paint on the butterflies in pastel glass paints. Allow to dry, and decorate the antennae and wings with gold or silver outliner.

Please refer to The Practical Workshop for full instructions on each technique.

Tiffany
lampshade

THE glow of a Tiffany-style lampshade on a dusky evening, shining out through the windows welcomes guests to your home in style.

These lamps are usually extremely expensive to buy and very complicated to make. They are crafted from lots of small and delicate pieces of glass, which give out a magical glow. If you can find a stained-glass pattern book for lamps it will give you plenty of ideas of what to incorporate in your design. Flowers, dragonflies and insects were the major design themes for Tiffany lampshades and these are all easy subjects to find or draw. Depending on what particular design you are using, the colours of the lamp should harmonize and complement your room. You can either decorate a recycled old glass shade or a new one from any major DIY or lighting store. You can even use a glass bowl and hang it from chains soldered to the rim using the copper-foil border method.

This project is photographed on p86

MATERIALS

wisteria design from pattern library (page 123)

glass hanging lampshade, preferably plain

black or leaded outliner

glass paints

stick-on lead tape

glass jewels, if required

glass glue

tracing paper or newsprint

double-sided tape

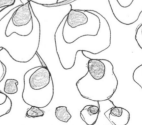

TO MAKE

1

Draw out the wisteria design onto tracing paper or white paper, preferably newsprint or something quite thin. Cut around the design, then fix it to the inside of the lampshade using double-sided tape. You may need to cut the design in places to make it fit the shape. Draw out the pattern using black outliner on the outside of the glass. Cover the entire glass with the pattern, moving it around to fill spaces. When the glass is covered with the design, check to see if it looks evenly distributed and add more flowers and leaves if necessary.

2

Select the wisteria colours and paint in the design. If you are using an old lamp that has coloured glass, you may need to paint on two coats of colour to eliminate base colour. Be careful to cover all of the surface, as any gaps will be obvious when the light is switched on. Let the project dry thoroughly.

3

Hold the lampshade up to the light to check for gaps and to see if any further definition would improve the appearance.

4

At this point, you can accentuate some of the major stalks and flowers using stick-on lead tape. The flowers centres can look stunning decorated with a glass jewel.

IMPORTANT

When the lamp is complete, check the electric connections carefully before rehanging.

Please refer to The Practical Workshop for full instructions on each technique.

Morning Glory
decanter & glasses

IMAGINE a glorious summer evening under the trees, with chilled white wine and glamorous flower-entwined glasses. These glasses will add an original statement to a summer party or make attractive ornaments to display in winter.

IDEAS FOR
THE HOME

You can often find water jugs and decanters very cheaply and it doesn't matter if they don't have matching glasses. Wine glasses are inexpensive and can bought in packs of four from any kitchenware store. However, I like to collect odd glasses at car-boot sales and yard sales so that there is always a collection of glasses to play with. Charity shops and jumble sales often have decanters, mostly pressed glass ones which, with a bit of titivation, become delightful subjects for this design.

This project is photographed on p101

MATERIALS

morning glory design from pattern library (page 122)

glass decanter or water jug, new or recycled

plain wine glasses

black and silver or gold outliner

glass paints

polyurethane varnish or clear glass paint

tracing paper

sticky tape

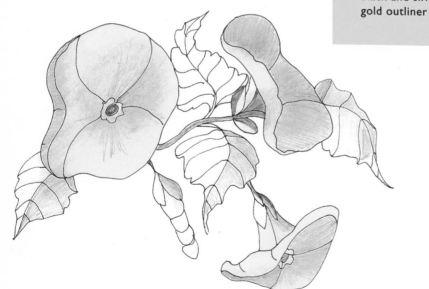

52

TO MAKE

Using the morning glory design, trace off the flowers and tape the paper to the inside of the glasses. Draw on the design with black outliner and leave to dry.

Paint in the flowers and leaves; you may find it easier to turn the glass up-side down to do this.

When dry, accentuate the centres of the flowers with silver or gold outliner. Be careful to leave a 5mm (¼ in) gap at the rim of the glass. Finish with a coat of varnish or clear glass paint. You can wash the glasses in cool soapy water if required, but they are not dishwasher safe.

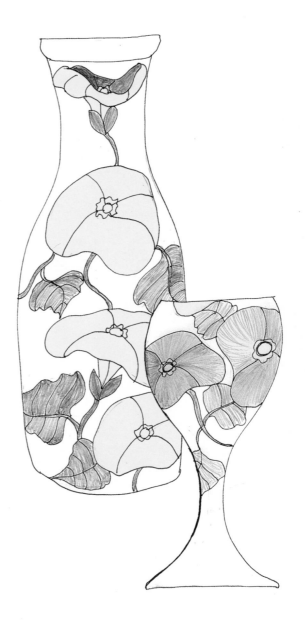

For the decanter, if the neck isn't wide enough to get the pattern inside and spread out, then the design will have to go on the outside either by the carbon paper method (see page 45) or, if you feel confident, draw it straight on to the glass. Either way, make sure that the flowers are evenly spaced around the decanter, adding some more if necessary.

Please refer to The Practical Workshop for full instructions on each technique.

Arthurian

g o b l e t s

THESE goblets painted in Gothic colours, embellished with jewels, would be perfectly at home in Camelot. The heavy dessert glasses with short stems have a deep refractive effect and a collection of these in front of a mirror lit by scented candles, and with a few perfect flowers might

IDEAS FOR THE HOME

get you an Oscar for stage design. Goblets that are used for ice-cream are really splendid for this design, and there are often trifle and sundae dishes in the same range. These will not break the bank as they usually come in sets and individually cost very little. Nightlights look great in them as well, especially when you display a collection of them all together.

Glass jewels of course just add to the magnificent effect and most of these glasses have flat facets on which to glue the jewels.

This project is photographed on p87

M A T E R I A L S

selection of dessert glasses or goblets

glass paints

flat-bottomed glass jewels

glass glue

gold and silver outliner

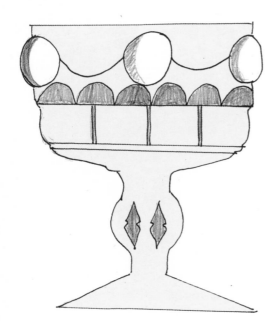

T O   M A K E

①

Put the goblets upside down on a flat surface lined with plenty of newspaper, as this procedure can be messy.

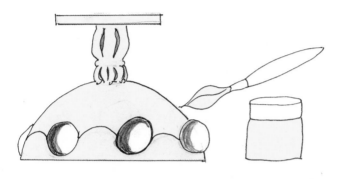

②

Select glass paint colours. Paint each goblet all over, starting from the top (the base) and working down in a spiral fashion. Allow to dry. (Do not paint the spots where you are going to glue jewels.)

③

Turn the goblets right side up and, starting from the top, work down the goblet creating swirls and blobs and twiddly bits using either the gold or silver outliner. Allow to dry. If you are using stick-on glass jewels, now is the time to glue them on.

④

If desired, place nightlights in the goblets, and group them in front of a window or a mirror to keep reflecting the inner colours.

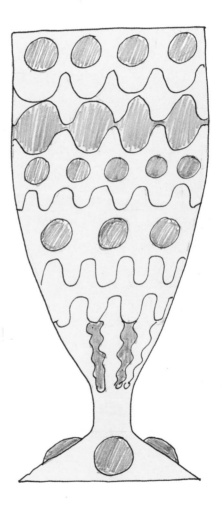

Please refer to The Practical Workshop for full instructions on each technique.

Fairy lantern

AN original way to welcome your guests, and let them know where you live, is to create a magic fairy lantern incorporating the number of your house. I have a large old-fashioned lantern high up on the corner of my house and I have removed the glass panels in the sides and painted them

with fairies. As we don't have a street number, I have painted in the house name instead.

In the summer the clematis winds its tendrils around the lamp and makes an even more stunning effect, with delicate flowers outlined against the light. You can use an old lantern or buy a new one from a hardware store or electrical outlet. Check to see if the panels are removable before you buy a new one. You can of course paint directly onto the lantern, but it's much easier if you remove the panels first and paint them horizontally.

This project is photographed on p90

MATERIALS

fairy design from pattern library (page 124)

lantern with glass panels

letter or number patterns for address

black outliner

glass paints

clear glass paint varnish or polyurethane varnish

TO MAKE

1

Remove the glass panels from the lantern and clean thoroughly.

2

Select the fairy design and make your arrangement for lettering.

3

Place the glass over the design and draw over it with black outliner. The glass-painted side should be on the inside. When the outliner is dry, paint in the design with glass paints.

4

Varnish with three coats of varnish, especially if, as I do, you live near the sea. Clean well with glass cleaner and replace the glass in the lantern.

Please refer to The Practical Workshop for full instructions on each technique.

THE CRAFT OF
painting on
GLASS

Section 3
RECYCLED
TREASURES

Decorative
c a n d l e h o l d e r s

MANY olive oil bottles are highly decorative with pretty upper sections in patterned glass, and they make ideal candleholders.

You can paint ordinary household candles with toning shade of glass paint to match. Using gold and silver outliner to accentuate the patterns on the bottle, lifts these candlesticks up into the realms of designer chic, and the added bonus here is that when the candles are lit, the bases also glow in the reflected light.

Many supermarkets sell attractive olive oil bottles, but if you can't find them try looking in specialist cook shops. Of course, the bottles must be well washed to get rid of any grease. I have found that the best method is to put them in the dishwasher, but a long soak in some very hot water and detergent is usually adequate.

This project is photographed on p107

M A T E R I A L S	
clean olive oil bottles	gold and silver outliner
glass paints	household candles

T O   M A K E

Select the colours to be used and carefully paint the bottles all over with solid colour except for the patterned zones. Leave to dry.

Take the gold or silver outliner and add decorative dots, swirls and borders around the bottle, following the lines of the glass patterns.

❸

Insert the candle in the neck of the bottle and paint with glass paint to match the bottle. You can also decorate the candles with the gold or silver outliner – these look wonderful when lit and grouped together on a dining table.

Please refer to The Practical Workshop for full instructions on each technique.

Cameo Fuchsia
bottles

THERE are, circulating the world, millions of glass bottles that are green, yellow, brown and blue. I have only once seen a purple bottle, which I rapidly transformed into a candlestick. These coloured bottles can become lovely cameo-style treasures by painting them in pale pastel tones. Pale green lilies on a dark-green glass bottle are lovely and pale bluebells on a background of dark-blue glass is also quite breathtaking. If you come across one of those gadgets for cutting bottles and converting them into glasses, you can make a matching bottle and glass set.

This project is photographed on p107

MATERIALS

fuchsia design
from pattern library
(page 124)

dark-coloured
green bottles

silver outliner

glass paint, white
plus blue or green

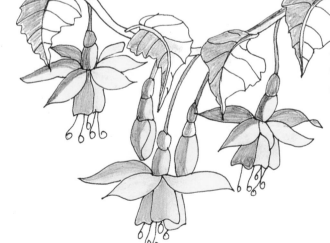

Please refer to The Practical Workshop for full instructions on each technique.

TO MAKE

1

Draw the fuchsia pattern onto the glass with silver outliner, either free-hand or by making a stencil, taping it to the bottle, and drawing round the inside edge of the stencil with outliner.

2

Mix white glass paint and a small amount of colour and paint in the flowers and leaves.

3

Accentuate the stamens and stems of the leaves with silver outliner.

Victorian Découpage
bottles

THIS project involves teaming two crafts together: découpage and glass painting. I wanted to create a pattern featuring the colour and clarity of glass plus the richness of flowers. Coming across some rather lovely Victorian-style rose wrapping paper I decided to cut out the roses and leaves and stick them over the glass-painted bottle. Then, with some carefully cut-out paper lace doilies placed strategically between the roses, all that was left was to use some gold outliner for the stems. I used four coats of polyurethane matt varnish to seal and finish the surface, carefully rubbing down the edges of paper between each coat. Add a gorgeous ribbon bow and the Victorian découpage bottle is ready for a candle or an arrangement of dried flowers.

MATERIALS

wrapping paper, wallpaper, or garden catalogues with suitable flower designs

clean glass jars or wine bottles, the larger the better

glass paints

paper doilies in gold and silver

gold or silver outliner

clear glass paint or polyurethane varnish

découpage varnish or matt polyurethane varnish

scissors

fine sandpaper

This project is photographed on p111

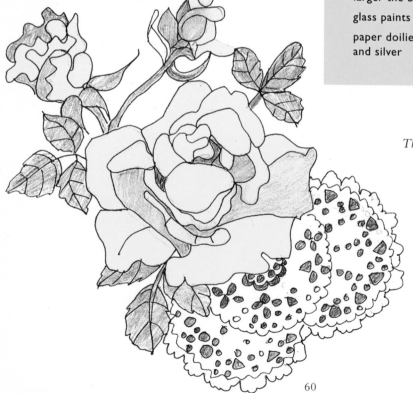

T O   M A K E

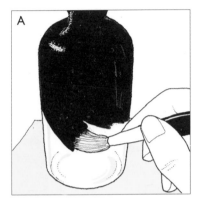

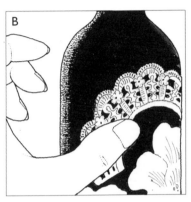

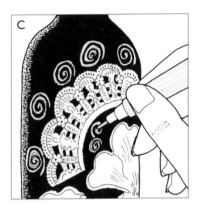

1

Cut out roses with leaves and buds as well as small rosettes from doilies.

2

Paint the bottle all over with your chosen colour of paint. Start at the top of the bottle and work downwards in a spiral, using little strokes (Fig. A). Choose Victorian colours such as amethyst, rose pink or Bristol blue. Make sure that the workplace is well covered with newspaper as this can be a messy operation.

3

While the glass paint is tacky, arrange the cut out roses over the glass painted bottle and press down well.

4

Stick the doily rosettes in between the roses. Press down well, making sure that there are no corners sticking up (Fig. B).

5

When dry, use the silver and gold outliner to outline the edge of the roses. You can also use the outliner as a design tool and add some swirly bits in between the roses (Fig. C).

6

Varnish two or three times with découpage varnish or polyurethane matt varnish. Rub down the edges of the paper gently between coats with fine sandpaper.

7

When dry, arrange some dried roses or grasses or tie a beautiful ribbon around the neck and place in window light or in front of a Victorian-style mirror.

Please refer to The Practical Workshop for full instructions on each technique.

Rainbow
n i g h t l i g h t s

LIGHT shining through a rainbow always looks dazzling and attractive and these nightlight holders look especially effective when you group together several different-sized jars. Honey jars are a good shape to use, and so are pickled onion, gherkin and big mayonnaise jars. It is a good idea to begin a glass collection if you have the room, so that you always have a selection of different shapes and sizes to hand. (After a while you become the person hanging around the bottle bank waiting to grab interesting glass bottles and jars before they are consigned to an environmental rebirth!)

Citronella candles are ideal for summer outdoor parties to keep the insects at bay and, instead of nightlights, these gaily painted jars can be filled with sweets or bath salts. They go like hot cakes at school and church fetes. They also make a colourful display area for dark and dingy window sills or those windows that are too high up to see out of but need some decorative touch.

MATERIALS

clean glass jars, washed and grease free

masking tape

felt-tip pen

glass paints

nightlights

This project is photographed on p108

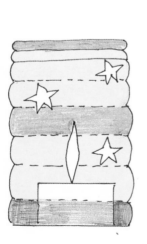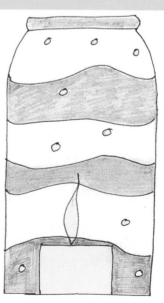

TO MAKE

1

Decide where to start your rainbow design. Divide the jar into seven sections - one for each colour of the rainbow - and lightly mark with a felt-tip pen.

2

Mask off each colour with masking tape and paint a section at a time, allowing twenty minutes between each colour. The colour should be slightly blurred at the borders.

3

Before the paint dries, and when it is still fairly tacky, press on some paper gold stars to add a little extra sparkle. Alternatively, add tiny dots with gold or silver outliner.

4

Disguise the screw-top necks of the bottles with gold or silver outliner designs. When completely dry, add a nightlight, sweets or dried flowers.

IMPORTANT

Do not ever paint on the inside of the jar as the glass paint is flammable!

Please refer to The Practical Workshop for full instructions on each technique.

Seaside Magic
bottles

COLLECT and wash interestingly shaped bottles; clear ones offer the best opportunity to be creative. Make sure that they are free from grease and quite dry. Shells are easy to come by and if you don't live near the beach, home decoration stores and mail-order craft suppliers often sell bags of shells, which you can paint gold for this project or incorporate into one of the other projects for decorated mirrors. If you gather shells from the beach, wash them in a mild solution of bleach to remove any biological material.

This project is photographed on p85

TO MAKE

Paint the bottle all over with blue glass paint and dab on green and blue colour highlights in wave-like lines around the body of the bottle. Leave to dry and, meanwhile, paint the cork and shell with gold paint. Use a model paint as it is quick drying and the gold doesn't tarnish.

Using the gold outliner, draw on stars, moons and, if you're artistic, sea horses and allow to dry. Stick extra gold stars and moons all over the bottle.

Please refer to The Practical Workshop for full instructions on each technique.

Glue the shell to top of the cork and insert in the bottle. Make some wavy lines and blobs around the neck of the bottle to disguise the screw-top marks.

④

Place in a well-lit window or on a shelf in front of a mirror, or even around the bath with scented candles and pieces of coral.

MATERIALS

- interestingly shaped bottles
- glass paints, including blue and gold
- gold outliner
- cork to fit the bottle
- decorative shell that will fit the top of the cork
- glue
- stick-on gold paper stars and moons

Tiger Vases
and bottles

THIS is a great design for those long slim vases that turn up at jumble sales or that you may have hidden in the back of a cupboard since the fifties. Some even have little pointy claw-like feet that can be incorporated into the overall design. You don't have to choose tiger stripes; spotty cheetah or giraffe patches look equally interesting. These glass objects are so spiky and animalistic it is hard to imagine them with flowers but they do look great with dried foliage and grasses or bits of twisted driftwood, artistically arranged in them.

This project is photographed on p98

MATERIALS

tall narrow glass vase (or bottle)

glass paints: yellow, brown and black

gold outliner

TO MAKE

Turn the vase or bottle upside down and paint all over with yellow paint. Wait twenty minutes until the paint is tacky. Paint in brown tiger stripes all down the length of the vase. Make them jagged and uneven, and allow to dry for ten minutes.

Carefully draw in thin black stripes in the centre of the brown stripes. The glass paints will mingle quite well, and evolve into quite animalistic patterns.

Please refer to The Practical Workshop for full instructions on each technique.

When dry, turn upright, decorate the rim of the vase with gold outliner and make little gold paw prints up and down the vase.

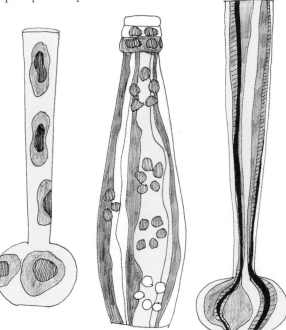

Top-Leaded
storage jars

THIS is a particularly good design for lidded jars which can be used for sweets or bathsalts, or filled with plain glass marbles as a stunning table decoration or paperweight. Plain coffee jars are also a good shape, and so are gravy and sauce jars. For references look in garden catalogues

as they often have excellent illustrations of fruit and flowers. A quick visit to the photocopy machine and you have a terrific pattern to use for your project. Alternatively kitchen wallpapers and wrapping papers often feature well-designed fruit that would adapt to make simple, clear patterns.

These jars are very popular at craft shows and fundraising events and look very impressive grouped together.

MATERIALS

fruit and flower design from pattern library (page 125), or create your own from wrapping paper, wallpaper or garden catalogues

glass jars, washed and grease free

black, gold and silver outliner

glass paints

reel of stick-on lead

tracing paper

masking tape

felt-tip pen

clear glass paint or polyurethane varnish

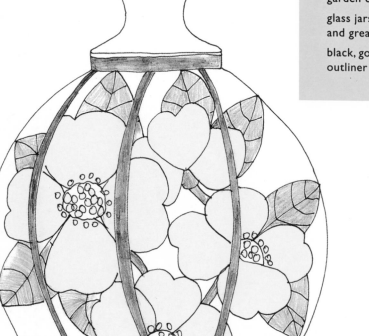

This project is photographed on p110

TO MAKE

1

Trace off the fruit and flower design and experiment with the pattern on the glass jar. When you know where you want the design to be, cut out and tape the paper inside the jar with masking tape so that it shows through the glass.

2

Draw over the pattern on the outside of the jar with black outliner and leave to dry.

3

Paint one side of the jar and leave to dry, turning the jar around to complete painting.

4

Decide on a leading design, such as diamonds or squares, and lightly mark on the jar with a felt-tip pen. Apply lead strips. Finish off the project by tightly wrapping the neck of the jar with lead strip to cover the screw-top marks.

TIP

When painting a jar, it is a good idea to prop the jar between scrunched up paper rolls to hold it steady, so you have a horizontal surface to work on.

5

Varnish with clear glass paint or polyurethane varnish if the jar is going to live in a bathroom or kitchen.

Please refer to The Practical Workshop for full instructions on each technique.

Impressionist
p o t s

IF you get a chance to look at any of the Monet waterlily paintings, you will see that the water is an astonishing collection of colours, all swirling about amid the lily pads. Take a piece of paper and some paints (watercolours or gouache) and see how many different colours and shades you can recreate from one small square of the painting. Make quite a few of these as reference points to use when creating your own Impressionist pots. I found a whole collection of old glass jars and bottles, which had been very discoloured because they had been sitting in a box for fifty years at the back of the garden shed. Having failed to get them clean and clear, I was wondering what to do with them.

Then, while I was looking at a Monet window panel, inspiration came! I decided to paint them all white first, then add the colour afterwards. Because I painted the colours on while the white was still tacky, the colours diffused, creating instant and original masterpieces. Each pot or jar was different and had delightful striations of colour running through the overall designs.

This project is photographed on p111

RECYCLED TREASURES

M A T E R I A L S

assortment of glass
jars and pots

glass paints

newspaper

T O   M A K E

1

Turn the pots upside down and place on top of newspapers. Paint pots with white glass paint, starting at the top, and leave to dry for 20 minutes (Fig. A).

2

Select the palate of colours to be used on each pot, and dab on very small amounts of the colours, starting at the top, with the pots still upside down. Leave the colours to move and flow and create the design (Fig. B).

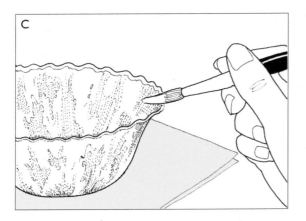

3

Leave to dry, turn over the pots and touch up the rims with white glass paint (Fig. C).

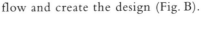

Please refer to The Practical Workshop for full instructions on each technique.

THE CRAFT OF
painting on
GLASS

Section 4

GIFTS FOR
FAMILY
& FRIENDS

Magic Eye mobile

ALL over the world, many cultures have adopted the symbol of the eye as a magic protector and bringer of good fortune. This magic eye makes a delightful present to wish someone happy birthday, good luck or even congratulations in a new home or job. The impact of the design lies with the colours and you can make it a very personal gift for someone if you match it to the colour of their own eyes.

GIFTS FOR FAMILY & FRIENDS

I have made a whole window of coloured eyes, quite small ones, and they look magnificent if there is a breeze to twirl them about. Hanging them on coloured cords or ribbons looks good, especially if you can find some co-ordinating glass jewels to use for the iris of the eye. On this pattern I have included the eye lashes and eye brows, but using just the eyeball can be equally effective.

This project is photographed on p92

MATERIALS

magic eye design from pattern library (page 126)	glass jewels
	glass glue
	copper foil
small glass roundels or ovals, Flemish glass if possible	solder and flux
	brass curtain ring
black outliner	co-ordinating cord or ribbon
glass paints	

TO MAKE

1
Enlarge or reduce the eye design to fit your glass oval or roundel. Place the glass over the pattern and draw with black outliner.

2
Paint in lashes and eyebrow and iris if you are not using glass jewels.

3
Arrange glass jewels within iris of eye, radiating out in a pattern. Glue in place.

4
Carefully wrap foil around the edge, brush on flux and solder.

5
Select a brass curtain ring and solder to the top of the eye roundel or oval. Attach a length of cord or ribbon. Clean the roundel and hang in a window to catch the light.

Please refer to The Practical Workshop for full instructions on each technique.

Christening
r o u n d e l

THIS is an original idea for a new arrival: a hand-painted roundel to hang in the nursery window, with the name and date of birth and appropriate decorations to suit that special new baby.

Apart from the obvious colours of blue and pink, parental and family ties can provide

fascinating background. One couple I knew were Australian and Mexican, so the roundel sported a little kangaroo in a Mexican hat underneath their national flags. Quite something to explain in fifty years time! Ducklings and rabbits are very popular as are baby elephants,

puppies and kittens. The traditional motifs of storks and bows and delicate flowers look really pretty when carried out in pale pastel colours, high-lighted with silver outliner.

This project is photographed on p99

M A T E R I A L S

2 x 30 cm (12 in) diameter glass roundels in 3 mm thick Flemish or float glass

glass paint

small piece of fabric or lace from christening gown or baby dress

dried gypsophila flowers (also known as baby's breath)

copper foil

solder and flux

chain

glass paints

outliner

pink or blue ribbon

felt-tip pen

pair of compasses

TO MAKE

Use a compass to mark a 3cm (1 in) border on each roundel and draw in with a felt-tip pen. Paint both borders in blue or pink, or whatever you choose.

Arrange a design in the centre of one roundel (paint-side down), incorporating the fabric of the gown and perhaps some flowers, together with the dried gypsophila. Leave some space for the baby's name and date of birth.

Place the second roundel, paint-side up over the first roundel and draw on the flowers from the christening roundel pattern when the material has been properly arranged.

Tape the two glass roundels together firmly with the copper foil, flux and solder and attach the chain.

Please refer to The Practical Workshop for full instructions on each technique.

Clean the surface of the glass and carefully paint in the flowers and draw on the name and date of birth, using outliner.

Attach the blue or pink ribbon where the chain joins the roundel.

Wedding-Day roundel

THIS project is based on those keepsake boxes that people use to display mementos from a special day. Of course all the items have to fit between two sheets of glass, so for a wedding roundel a selection of the following might be suitable: the invitation, a piece of the wedding gown, pieces of the bridesmaid's gowns, some flowers from the church, bouquets, napkins, cocktail umbrellas, the bridegroom's tie, the honeymoon hotel brochure and so on. The idea is to create a fascinating collage to surround the inscription giving the names and dates. This idea can be used for all sorts of memorable occasions: graduations, birthdays, engagements, in fact you would be surprised how amazing all these little mementos look when arranged for a purpose.

This project is photographed on p97

MATERIALS

2 x 30 cm (12 in) diameter, 2 mm thick, glass roundels	copper foil
	solder and flux
black and silver outliner	glass paint
	chain
assortment of wedding mementos	masking tape

TO MAKE

1

Place one roundel on a flat surface. Find its centre, and write in with outliner the names and dates: try to keep the wording as compact and centred as you can. (It can be helpful to do a rough on paper first.)

2

Arrange items closely around the wording. If it is a problem to keep them in place, use a tiny dab of glue to anchor the objects.

3

Place the second roundel on top and, using masking tape, lightly tape together.

4

Foil, flux and solder the edges of the roundels, and clean the surface of the glass. Then, using silver outliner, carefully draw a decorative pattern around the edge of the second roundel using an appropriate motif if possible.

Please refer to The Practical Workshop for full instructions on each technique.

5

If you feel it would improve the appearance, at this point you can add some flowers or wedding bells with outliner and glass paint.

6

Attach the chain and clean with glass cleaner.

Angel
tree ornaments

THESE make lovely and unusual gifts, especially in sets, perhaps one angel for each member of the family. I like to make them all one colour. They look wonderful hung in the window at Christmas or twinkling on the tree or even hanging on a suction cup-hook in the back of the car.

At other times of the year you could make fairies instead of angels, but I find that guardian angels are always popular, especially as a gift to a new driver. I've made guardian angels for most of my friends' birthdays this year and they have been quite a hit. Some have been themed on the recipient's favourite sport or activity and some look vaguely like their owner.

This project is photographed on p90

MATERIALS

angel design from pattern library (page 126)	silver, gold and black outliner
	glass paints
7.5 cm (3 in) diameter roundels, float or Flemish glass	copper foil
	brass curtain rings
	silver or gold cord

TO MAKE

Using the angel patterns, draw the designs onto the roundels with black outliner. Leave to dry and paint carefully.

2

When dry, decorate wings and halos with gold or silver outliner, and leave to dry.

3

Wrap the edges with foil. Solder a curtain ring to the top of the roundel. Attach gold or silver cord to the ring, knot and hang on the Christmas tree or in the window.

Please refer to The Practical Workshop for full instructions on each technique.

Nativity Scene
with mini-jars

NATIVITY scenes are always popular with children and here is a project that they can make themselves, for very little cost, which will look spectacular day or night. Start a collection of small glass jars well before Christmas, as they will all want to do this one. Collect different sizes,

GIFTS FOR
FAMILY &
FRIENDS

including fish-paste jars for sheep and pigs. There is no need to build a stable, as in most cases these figures look best on a windowsill or mantelpiece.

This project is photographed on p102

M A T E R I A L S

nativity scene designs
from pattern library
(page 127)

assorted small jars

black, gold and silver
outliner

glass paint

nightlights

T O   M A K E

Select the correct-shaped jars to represent the nativity characters from the pattern library.

Draw on faces and robes with black outliner and leave to dry. Paint on the robes and details with glass paint.

When dry, arrange on a windowsill or in front of a mirror. At night, they look wonderful illuminated with candles or white fairy lights.

Please refer to The Practical Workshop for full instructions on each technique.

Christmas
nightlights

GIFTS FOR FAMILY & FRIENDS

THE glow of candlelight through coloured glass gives the festive table or mantelpiece that magic touch. This idea incorporates glass painting and candle making and is a super way of recycling old glasses. They don't have to be anything special and there are lot of 1950s goblets still around that look terrific when painted and lit with candles. The actual creation of the candle itself isn't difficult and I have shown ten-year-olds how to do this quite successfully. This is a great project for Christmas fairs and fundraising events and, if you light one or two and put them in front of a mirror, they attract a lot of customers. You can use the same method with flower designs for summer dinner parties, and pumpkin designs for Halloween parties. A St. Valentine's party candle can be created by painting on ruby-red hearts all around the glass and using a pink candle. If you don't have one, then an ordinary household candle will do if you add some pink cake colouring to the melted wax.

This project is photographed on p90

MATERIALS

Christmas holly and candle designs from pattern library (page 128)

large brandy glasses

household candles

drinking straws

gold, silver and black outliner

glass paint

T O   M A K E

First, melt a candle, either in a saucepan or in a microwave.

Remove the wick, and pour the melted candlewax into the glass until three-quarters of the way up the sides.

2

Tie the wick around one end of a drinking straw and suspend in the candlewax until set. Untie, remove straw and trim to a suitable length.

3

Turn the glass upside down, and using Christmas holly and the candle design, draw on with black outliner.

4

When dry, paint in the design. Allow to dry thoroughly. Leave enough room for a 2cm (¾in) border around the glass rim.

5

Use gold or silver outliner to highlight the Christmas design and the rim of the glass.

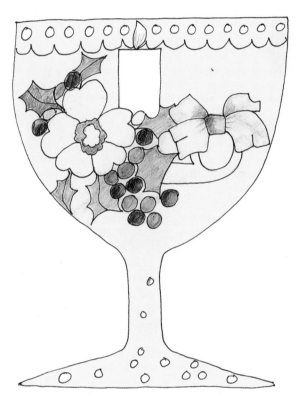

Please refer to The Practical Workshop for full
instructions on each technique.

$Easter\ Egg$ r o u n d e l

EASTER has its symbols: flowers, cakes, rabbits, lambs and of course eggs. But Easter is not celebrated in quite such an elaborate way as Christmas. We don't tend to decorate our homes with fairy lights, or hang glittery garlands on our front doors, but here is an easy project to hang in the window, to set the Easter scene. A collection of handsome painted-glass eggs in the window look really pretty in the spring sunshine, and twinkle away merrily on those still quite dark evenings. You could of course send them as Easter gifts and they have the added advantage of not being fattening.

GIFTS FOR FAMILY & FRIENDS

For the oval roundels, either get the glazier to cut these for you or use the glass insets from shop-made oval photo frames, and use the frames for needlework projects.

This project is photographed on p105

This project is photographed on p105

MATERIALS

Easter egg designs (or pattern library page 128)

six oval glass roundels

black and gold outliner

glass paints

copper foil

solder and flux

small brass curtain rings

narrow satin ribbon in green, pink and yellow

TO MAKE

Select some Easter egg designs or use the pattern library. Place the pattern under the glass ovals and draw over with outliner. Leave to dry.

Paint in Easter eggs in suitable spring colours

Foil, flux and solder the edges and solder a ring to each oval.

Please refer to The Practical Workshop for full instructions on each technique.

Cut lengths of ribbon and tie through the rings. Hang the eggs in a window to make a harmonious display.

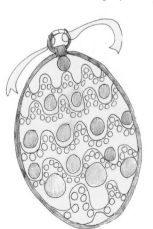

80

THE CRAFT OF
painting on
GLASS

gallery of
glass paintings

ABOVE: A vivid jungle scene is perfect for a panel designed to obscure an ugly view.

LEFT: The author at work in her conservatory-cum-studio.

ABOVE: Autumn leaves, pressed between
two pieces of glass make a stunning roundel.

RIGHT: Recycled bottles with a touch of
'seaside magic'.

ABOVE: The goblets, which would
grace the court of King Arthur, are decorated
with glass jewels.

LEFT: A humble shade is transformed into a
creation worthy of Tiffany.

ABOVE: A window panel inspired by Monet's waterlilies.

LEFT: A roundel is a charming and novel way to display the name of your house.

ABOVE: An old-fashioned oil lamp is transformed
by a painted daffodil design.

LEFT: A selection of tiny roundels adorn the tree,
with the fairy lantern and the
Christmas nightlight in the foreground.

ABOVE: A trio of magic eye mobiles will bring
good fortune *and* decorate a room.

RIGHT: The top leading using stick-on lead gives a
highly traditional stained-glass effect.

ABOVE: A panel suspended outside will catch and
reflect light throughout the day.

RIGHT: An old mirror is transformed with a
garland of fruit and flowers.

ABOVE: A selection of mock cranberry glass
can be made for much less than the price of the
real thing.

RIGHT: A personalised roundel makes a superb
commemoration for a special event.

ABOVE: A roundel to celebrate a new
arrival, with appropriate decorations and the
baby's name and date of birth.

LEFT: Any interesting vases or bottles can
be transformed with tiger stripes or cheetah's paw
marks.

ABOVE: A decanter and matching glasses painted
with a profusion of morning glory.

LEFT: A front-door panel with a rambling
California poppy design.

ABOVE: A complete nativity scene made from a
collection of tiny jars.

RIGHT: A dragon-design door panel embellished
with glass jewels.

A selection of glass paintings including the vibrant poppy roundel, the jewelled peacock roundel, the field mice roundel, the Easter egg roundel and the author's conservatory panels.

ABOVE: The author's conservatory-cum-studio
displaying a number of different projects
including painted bottles, roundels and mobiles.

RIGHT: vases and candle-holders made with
fuchsia and other floral designs.

ABOVE: A glass roundel inspired by the bridge
in Monet's garden at Giverny.

LEFT: Dramatic nightlights made from the
simplest jam jars.

ABOVE: Candleholders decorated with
paint and decoupage; 'impressionist' bottles
and pots in the foreground.

LEFT: A glass dome is turned into a
family heirloom with painted butterflies.
(Top-leaded storage jars behind.)

THE CRAFT OF
painting on
GLASS

pattern
library

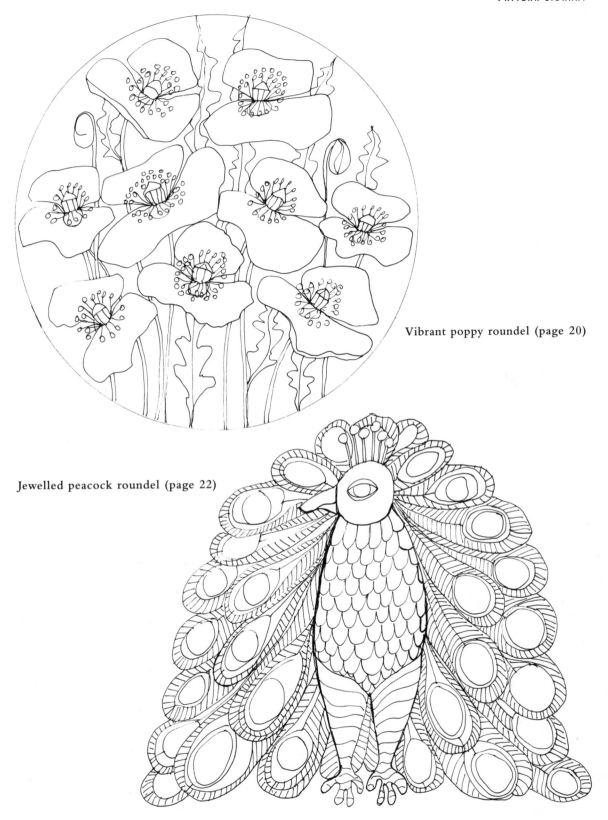

Vibrant poppy roundel (page 20)

Jewelled peacock roundel (page 22)

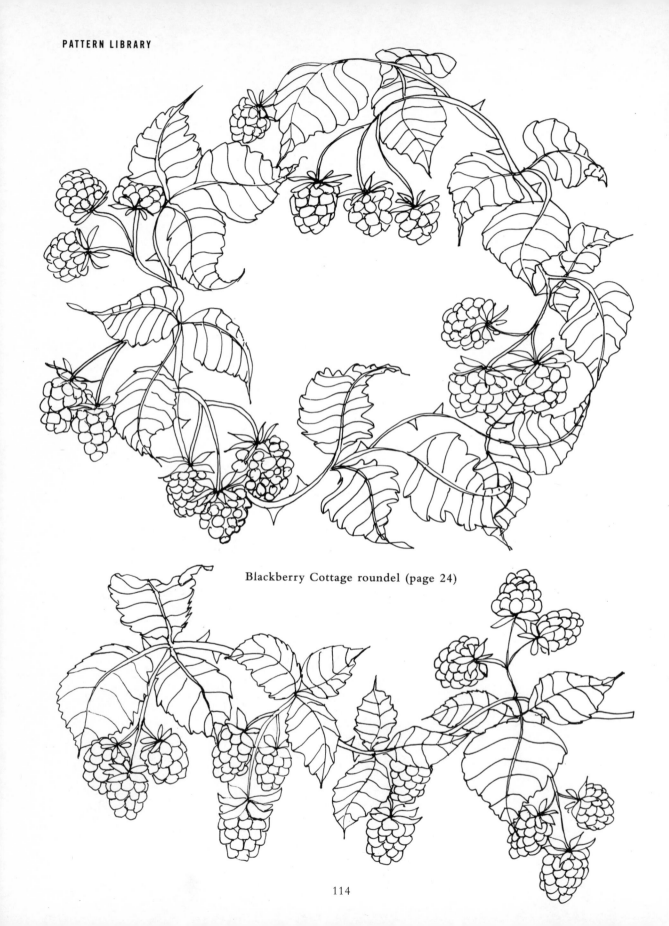

Blackberry Cottage roundel (page 24)

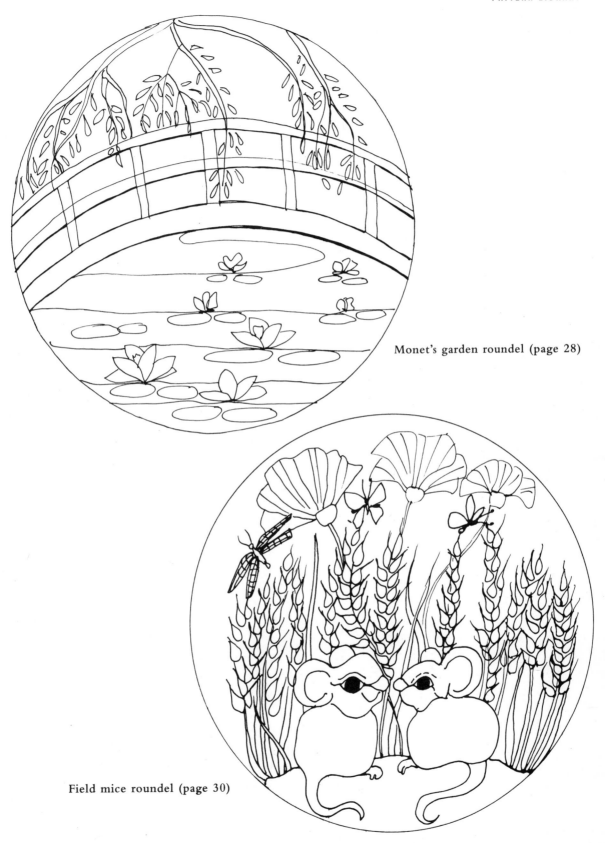

Monet's garden roundel (page 28)

Field mice roundel (page 30)

Jolly sailor sign (page 32)

Floral door panel (page 37)

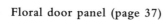

Jungle scene panel (page 34)

Tulip window panel (page 38)

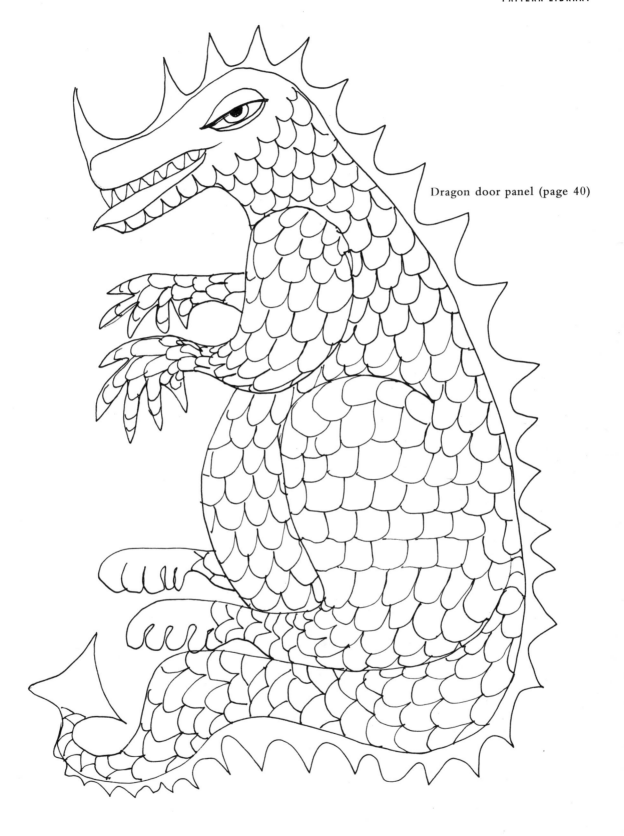

Dragon door panel (page 40)

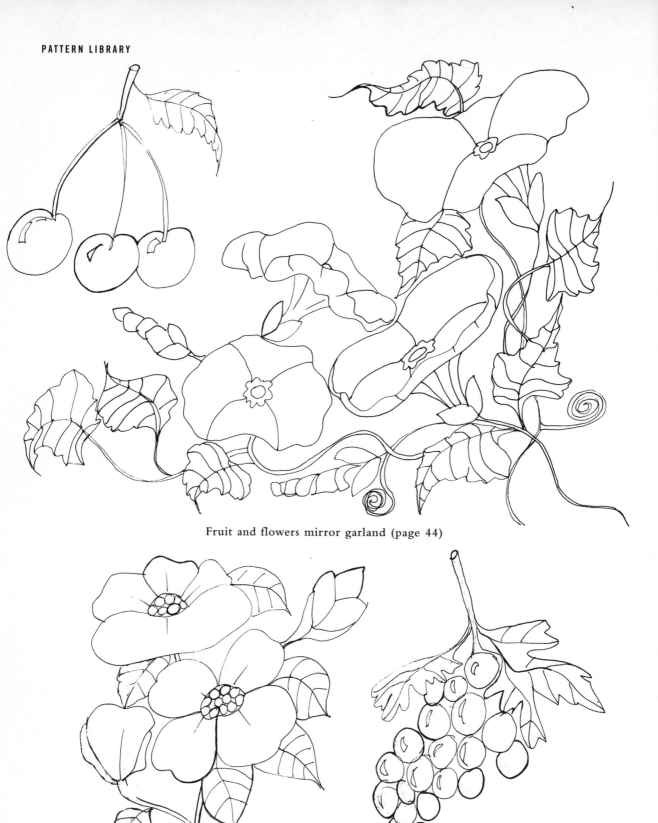

Fruit and flowers mirror garland (page 44)

Daffodil lamp (page 47)

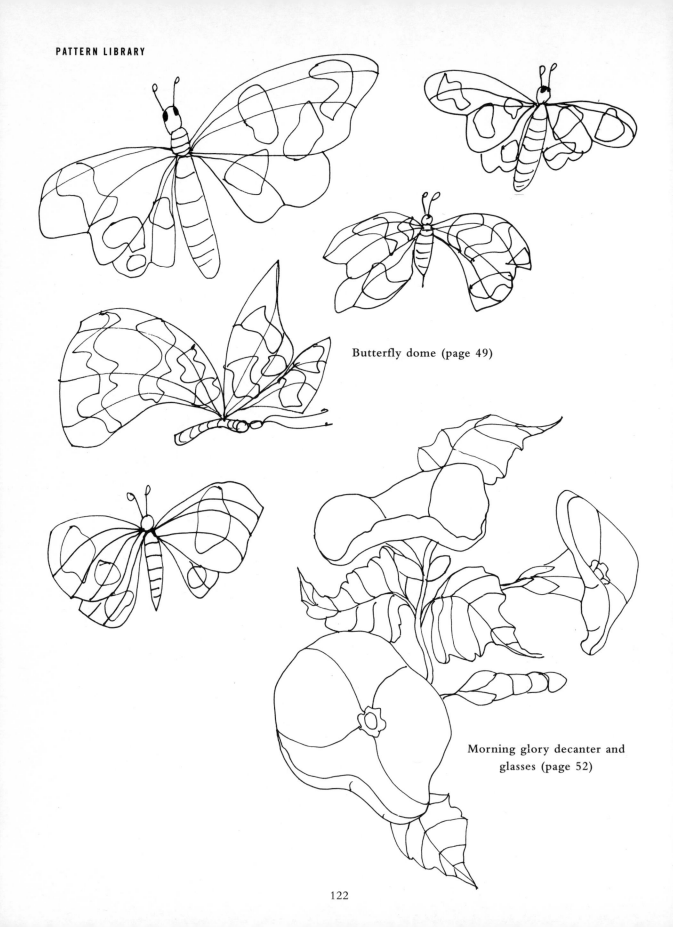

Butterfly dome (page 49)

Morning glory decanter and
glasses (page 52)

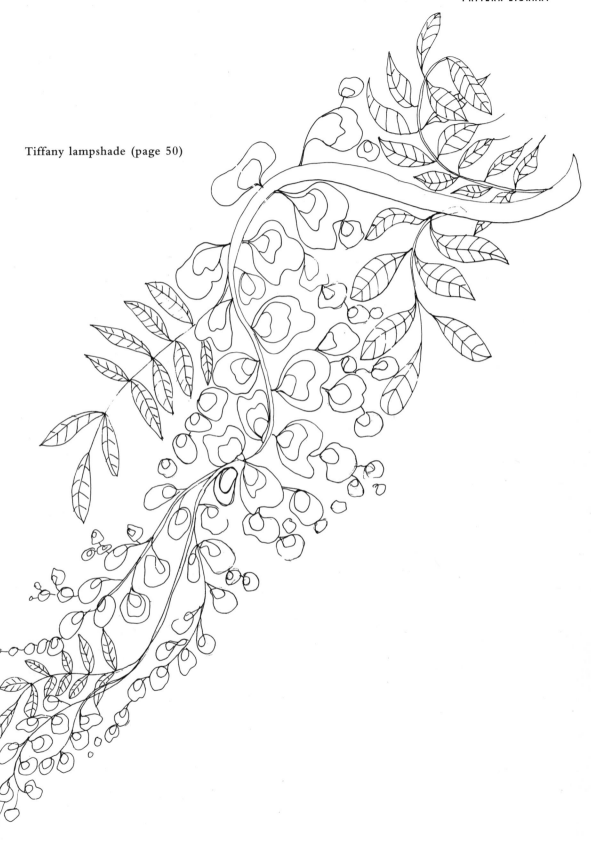

Tiffany lampshade (page 50)

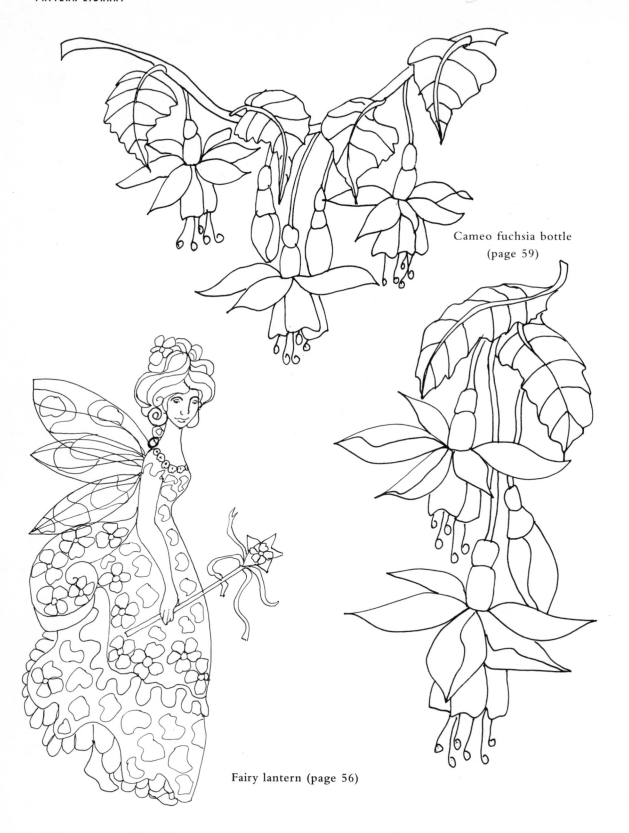

Cameo fuchsia bottle
(page 59)

Fairy lantern (page 56)

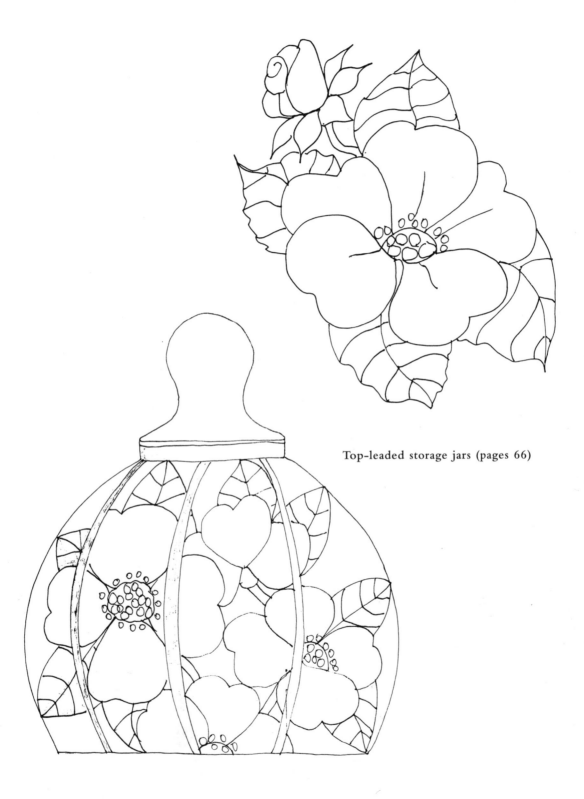

Top-leaded storage jars (pages 66)

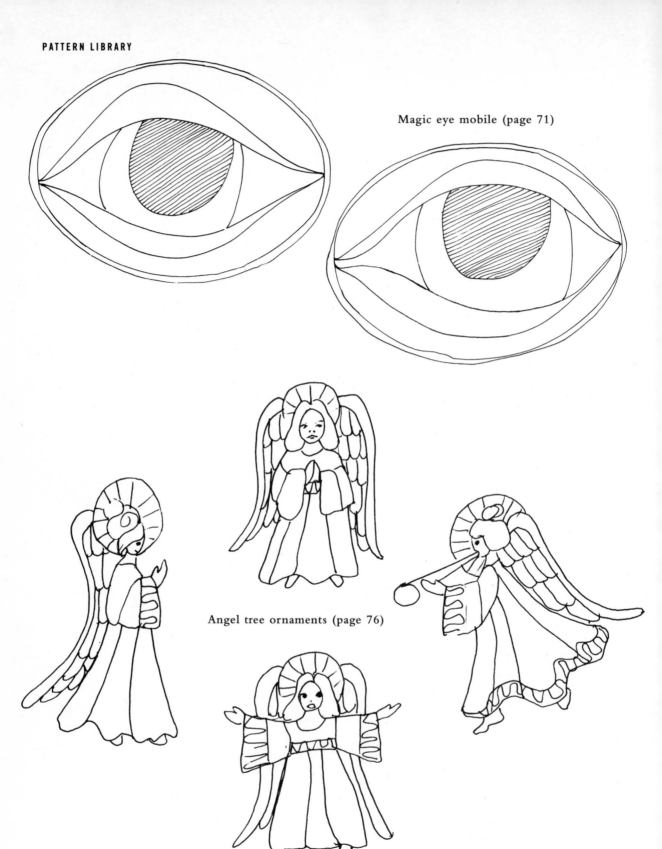

Magic eye mobile (page 71)

Angel tree ornaments (page 76)

Nativity scene with mini-jars (page 77)

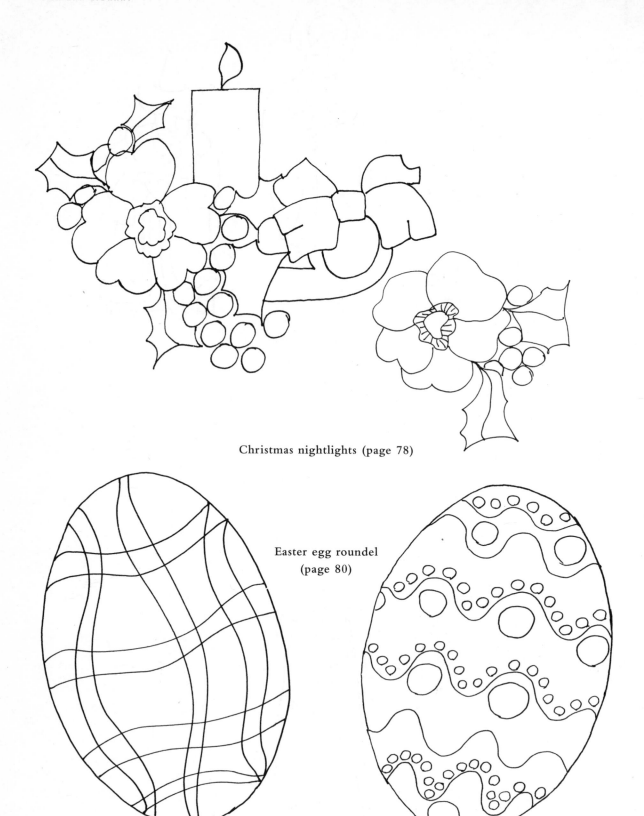

Christmas nightlights (page 78)

Easter egg roundel
(page 80)